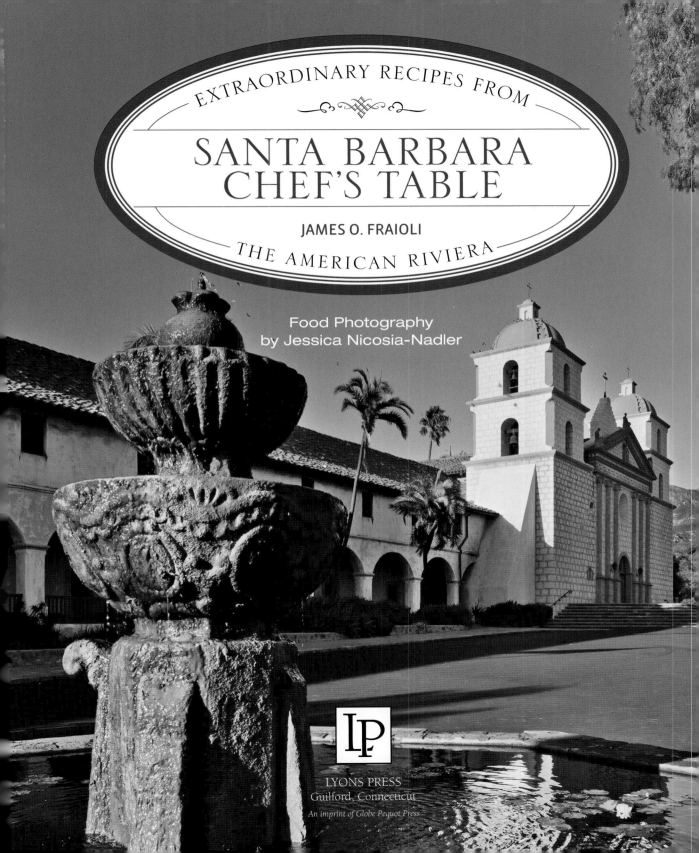

EXTRAORDINARY RECIPES FROM

SANTA BARBARA
CHEF'S TABLE

JAMES O. FRAIOLI

THE AMERICAN RIVIERA

Food Photography
by Jessica Nicosia-Nadler

LYONS PRESS
Guilford, Connecticut
An imprint of Globe Pequot Press

Lyons Press is an imprint of Globe Pequot Press.

Food photography by Jessica Nicosia-Nadler; see page 191 for complete photo credits

Text design: Libby Kingsbury
Layout artist: Nancy Freeborn
Project editor: Julie Marsh

Library of Congress Cataloging-in-Publication Data

Fraioli, James O., 1968-
 Santa Barbara chef's table : extraordinary recipes from the American Riviera / James O. Fraioli ; food photography by Jessica Nicosia-Nadler.
    p. cm.
 Includes bibliographical references and index.
 ISBN 978-0-7627-7358-9 (alk. paper)
1. Cooking, American—California style. 2. International cooking. 3. Cooking—California—Santa Barbara. 4. Restaurants—California—Santa Barbara—Guidebooks. I. Title.
 TX715.2.C34.F725 2012
 641.59794—dc23

                                                                                    2012008438

Printed in the United States of America

10 9 8 7 6 5 4 3 2 1

Restaurants and chefs often come and go, and menus are ever-changing.
We recommend you call ahead to obtain current information before
visiting any of the establishments in this book.

To the great city of Santa Barbara and the Santa Ynez Valley—thank you for being my home away from home.

Contents

Acknowledgments

James O. Fraioli would like to personally thank the following people for their generous support and assistance with this book.

Sagiri Arima and Kathleen Hansen for their countless hours of research, persistence, and dedication. Thank you as well, Nancy Ransohoff, for stepping in.

Award-winning food photographer Jessica Nicosia-Nadler, you continue to amaze and impress.

Chef John Hall and the extraordinary culinary team at Le Cordon Bleu College of Culinary Arts in Sacramento, California: Chef Richard W. Jensen II, Chef Robert Siegmund, Torrey Crable, Chef Eric Veldman-Miller, Chef Scot Rice, Chef Adrian Day-Murchison, Chef Josh Bogin, Chef Charlin Wright, Patricia Nicosia, Elaine Kelly, Phoebe Cansanay, Husan Brodders, Lilly Kovacs, Ashley Banning, Michael Martinez, and Lucas Nadler.

Mary Norris and editor extraordinaire Katie Benoit at Globe Pequot Press, longtime literary agent Andrea Hurst, and last, but certainly not least, all the contributing chefs and restaurants. Without your unbelievable support and assistance, this book would not have been possible.

Introduction

If there's one adjective that best describes Santa Barbara, the adjective is *breathtaking.*

Santa Barbara, also known as the American Riviera (because of its Mediterranean-like views and climate), lies just a two-hour drive north of Los Angeles. From the beautiful clean beaches to the stunning mountains to the colorful culture that resides within, Santa Barbara is a premier resort destination for visitors and a fairytale-like setting for those who call Santa Barbara home.

In 1542, Portuguese explorer João Rodrigues Cabrilho discovered California, along with Santa Barbara and the neighboring Channel Islands. Unfortunately, one year later, the famed sailor fell ill on nearby San Miguel Island, where he is buried. Before Cabrilho's arrival, the Chumash people populated the coastline, living off the land. Around the eighteenth century, Spanish Franciscan monks began arriving, as part of their mission-building venture through California. It wasn't until 1846, after twenty-four years of Mexican rule, that Santa Barbara finally became a US territory.

> *This is my invariable advice to people: Learn how to cook—try new recipes, learn from your mistakes, be fearless, and above all have fun!*
>
> —JULIA CHILD, one of Santa Barbara's
> most prominent residents and culinary icons

Many of today's historical sites and alluring architecture reflect the early inhabitants of Santa Barbara. The same holds true for the pre-Hollywood era of the early 1900s when the silent film industry arrived to the area. Filmmakers like Charlie Chaplin set up shop in Santa Barbara, as did actor Lon Chaney and Flying A Studios, which made about 1,200 films in the area, mostly Westerns.

Santa Barbara was also home to a unique culinary scene at the time because of a rich agricultural community harvesting an abundance of fresh fruits and vegetables. In neighboring Los Olivos, about a forty-minute drive north of Santa Barbara, Sides Hardware and Shoes welcomes travelers in droves. In the original building, now restored, the popular restaurant is known for its fine food and family atmosphere. It is led by award-winning chefs and brothers Jeff and Matt Nichols (who graciously contributed three recipes for this book).

Just like yesteryear, Santa Barbara County chefs and restaurants continue to work directly with local fishermen, farmers, and now winemakers (wine has been the most significant culinary boom in Santa Barbara in recent years, further encouraged by the Academy Award–winning film *Sideways*). Although the *Sideways* phenomenon is all but a distant memory, wine production in the area continues to reign supreme. In fact, in the town of Los Olivos, just north of Santa Barbara, dozens of tasting rooms cater to wine aficionados. According to many of the local tasting room managers, about 80 percent of the visitors are from Los Angeles, many of whom were unaware wine tasting was available in Santa Barbara County prior to the popular film. Today, wine tasting in Los Olivos has a permanent place on the map for culinary travelers.

And with great Santa Barbara wines comes great Santa Barbara food. Menus reflect the seasons (yes, there are seasons in California), celebrating artichokes, asparagus, and citrus in the spring; heirloom tomatoes, Mexican chiles, and luscious strawberries in the summer; and hearty root vegetables and wild mushrooms in the fall and winter. Eating local is definitely a Santa Barbara—and sustainable—way of life. The well-known Santa Barbara Farmers' Market, along with other farmers' markets, such as those in Montecito and Solvang, enables locals and visitors to shop for and learn about fresh ingredients, to begin eating healthy, and to support communities that believe in protecting and caring for Mother Earth.

In this book, forty of the best Santa Barbara County restaurants come together to dazzle you with delicious recipes while promoting a healthy farm-to-table way of life. The restaurants' owners all believe that high-quality food should always be on the table for family and friends to admire and appreciate. If you happen to be in Santa Barbara, experiencing these award-winning restaurants and culinary surprises firsthand should top your list of things to do. Several local magazines feature everything you need to know about dining in and around Santa Barbara, so if you're unsure of where to go or what to eat, pick up a copy (or visit the website) of *Santa Barbara Dining and Destinations* or *Santa Barbara Magazine*.

Many who visit Santa Barbara will begin the day strolling along a sandy beach, then enjoy a relaxed appetizer or starter at Bouchon, Bella Vista, or Montecito Cafe. For lunch, you might venture off the beaten path and explore one of the many culinary treasures hidden throughout the area, such as the famous San Ysidro Ranch, the historic and rustic Cold Spring Tavern, or the lauded Trattoria Uliveto, nestled to the north, in the little town of Orcutt. In Santa Barbara, it seems almost customary to stop and admire the sunset with drink in hand; two oceanfront properties that offer dazzling Pacific Ocean views and refreshing libations while the sun dips over the horizon are Brophy Brothers at the Santa Barbara harbor and the Santa Barbara Shellfish Company at the end of Stearns Wharf. Dining can be equally rewarding, and the lively pulse of State Street seems to attract the most attention, with such outstanding restaurants as Blue Agave, Ca'Dario, Jane, Kai Sushi, Opal, and the Palace Grill. For the premier dining experience, serious foodies will travel north along the scenic coast on Highway 101, or take a shortcut by driving over the winding mountain pass of the Chumash Highway, and attend one of the opulent winemaker dinners that take place at the wineries or at the sumptuous restaurants in town, including the Alisal Guest Ranch & Resort, the Ballard Inn, Brothers Restaurant—Sides Hardware and Shoes, the Hitching Post II, or the always-popular Trattoria Grappolo, where you can rub shoulders with movie stars, both past and present.

As you explore Santa Barbara County and the wonderful restaurants within—whether firsthand or through the pages of this book—keep in mind that many of the recipes have been modified for the home cook, making them more practical and user-friendly for the limited equipment of the average kitchen. Nevertheless, if you take your time, adjust as you go, and rely on farmers' markets to supply you with the freshest of herbs, spices, and ingredients, your finished dishes will be as radiant as the Santa Barbara sunshine!

APPETIZERS & SMALL PLATES

Santa Barbarans and those residing in the outlying communities believe in two vital necessities for fabulous tasting food—fresh ingredients and local purveyors. This healthy farm-to-table way of life not only unites diners with farmers but also ensures that good quality food is always on the table for family and friends to admire and appreciate.

Whether or not you live in Santa Barbara, fresh local ingredients are a great place to begin when thinking about dazzling dishes to prepare. And a visit to your neighborhood farmers' market is a must for finding what you will need. While there, you can buy direct from the farmers and obtain fresh, organic, and seasonal foods often produced a drivable distance from your home.

In this chapter, a collection of Santa Barbara–area restaurants showcase signature recipes featuring fresh local ingredients. Feel free to adapt the dishes to reflect your hometown and the wonderful ingredients offered in your region.

Santa Barbara's notable Bouchon starts it off by highlighting delectable California flavors with a savory Goat Cheese & Asian Pecan Tart, along with an exotic three-layer mushroom tower. Cava Restaurant & Bar takes advantage of the Spanish-influenced ingredients readily available in Santa Barbara and introduces two tapas-style nibbles: Tortilla Española and Gambas al Ajillo (hot and spicy garlic shrimp). Downey's showcases a Shell Bean Ragout, first introduced at a sit-down farm dinner, and a simple-to-make Lobster Flan, allowing East and West Coast cooks to use their local lobster. Emilio's Ristorante & Bar whips up a savory Goat Cheese & Gorgonzola Crostada, as well as a paella that incorporates fresh Santa Barbara seafood. The Hitching Post II pays homage to Santa Barbara County farmers with Smoked Duck & Grilled Corn Quesadillas and tender grilled artichokes and grilled pasilla peppers. Speaking of peppers, the Palace Grill, which offers Cajun cuisine in the heart of Santa Barbara, invites home cooks to try Jalapeño-Cheddar Corn Muffins, featuring, of course, fresh chile peppers, as well as Louisiana Barbecue Shrimp. And Petros Los Olivos Restaurant cashes in on the local produce craze with a delectable trio of fresh herb- and vegetable-laden appetizers and small plates.

BOUCHON

9 WEST VICTORIA STREET, SANTA BARBARA
(805) 730-1160
WWW.BOUCHONSANTABARBARA.COM
OWNER: MITCHELL SJERVEN

Santa Barbara County has become famous for its wines. One of the most charming places to sip and savor such wines while enjoying a delicious meal is behind the aromatic hedge at Bouchon.

Specializing in California wine country cuisine, Bouchon uses ingredients that are always fresh and always of the highest quality. They're sourced locally, from the ripe fruits and bright vegetables collected at the Santa Barbara farmers' market, to the wild sustainable seafood hauled in by fishermen off the Pacific Coast. Diners at Bouchon enjoy signature dishes including roast duck, salade lyonnaise, and French onion soup, and other savory creations, such as rich and buttery foie gras and tarte au chèvre. The waitstaff at Bouchon is friendly and cordial, and the atmosphere is warm and inviting. The door is always open—literally—so come in and enjoy a glass of wine (there are more than fifty kinds to choose from) and a delicious meal, whether a lunch on the plant-adorned patio, a candlelit dinner, or to celebrate a special event (for anniversaries, Bouchon will litter your table with rose petals).

The wine list, of course, is extensive—featuring locally produced California Chardonnay, Pinot Noir, and Syrah, among others—and perfectly paired with the restaurant's dishes. If you're unsure of what wine to order, the staff are always available to suggest a varietal that will enhance each menu item. Each wine, particularly the local varieties, reflects the quality and character of the region and works in harmony with the cuisine.

GOAT CHEESE & ASIAN PECAN TART

SERVES 4

Pecan pastry dough:

1 cup toasted pecans, finely chopped
¼ cup sugar, divided
2 large eggs, whisked
1 teaspoon salt
2 cups all-purpose flour
2 sticks cold butter

Tart filling:

¼ cup pecans, finely chopped
2 medium shallots, peeled and finely diced
2 cups goat cheese
½ cup mascarpone
¼ cup peeled and diced Asian pear
½ cup crème fraîche
1 teaspoon chopped fresh Italian parsley
1 teaspoon chopped fresh thyme, chopped

Pear vinaigrette:

¼ cup pear vinegar (available at specialty markets)
¾ cup extra-virgin olive oil
Salt and freshly ground black pepper, to taste

Salad:

6 ounces frisée
6 ounces arugula

Preheat the oven to 325°F.

To make the pecan pastry dough, put the pecans and 1 teaspoon sugar in a food processor and pulse. Transfer to a stand mixer with paddle attachment. Add the remaining sugar and mix on low. Add the eggs, salt, flour, and butter. Mix until a dough forms. Remove dough from mixer bowl and knead dough on a flat work surface. Using a ring mold, cut out disks from the dough, which will become the tartlet cups. Place the disks on a greased cookie sheet and bake in the preheated oven for about 12–15 minutes, or until golden. Remove from oven, set aside and let cool

Increase the oven temperature to 350°F.

To make the tart filling, combine the pecans, shallots, goat cheese, mascarpone, Asian pear, crème fraîche, parsley, and thyme in a bowl. Mix (either by hand or using a stand mixer) for about 1 minute, or until blended. Fill the baked tartlet cups with the filling mix. Bake for 7–10 minutes.

To make the pear vinaigrette, combine the pear vinegar, olive oil, and salt and pepper in a small mixing bowl. Whisk until well blended. (The dressing can be made in advance and chilled.)

To make the salad, toss the greens with the vinaigrette in a mixing bowl. Evenly divide the greens among four salad plates, placing them on one side. The warm tarts can be served to the side of the salad or resting against the greens.

Exotic Mushroom Mille-Feuilles

SERVES 2

1 pound heirloom cherry tomatoes
2 pounds exotic mushrooms (oyster, shiitake,
  hen of the woods, porcini, morels,
  trumpet royals, etc.)
¼ cup chopped white onion
¼ cup chopped leeks
1 package phyllo (puff pastry) dough
1 tablespoon olive oil
2 tablespoons minced shallot
1 tablespoon minced garlic
½ cup snow peas
½ cup julienne-cut asparagus
2/3 cup white wine
1/8 cup lemon juice
2 tablespoons chopped fresh herbs (parsley,
  sage, rosemary, thyme)
3 tablespoons butter
Pecorino Tartufo cheese, shaved, for garnish

Begin by roasting the cherry tomatoes in a preheated 350°F oven for approximately 1½ hours. When the tomatoes start to become wrinkled, remove them from the oven. Leave oven on.

To make mushroom stock, clean the mushrooms, collecting all the mushroom scraps you trim. Add the scraps, along with the chopped onion and leeks, to a small pot of water (about 2 cups) over medium-low heat. Simmer for about 45 minutes. You'll need about 3/8 cup mushroom stock. Set aside.

Meanwhile, cut the phyllo dough into six 4- to 5-inch disks and place them on a greased baking sheet. Weight the disks by placing another baking sheet on top. Bake until the dough is crispy, about 10 minutes.

Coat a medium-size sauté pan with olive oil. Over medium-high heat, add the shallots, garlic, and mushrooms. Sauté until the vegetables are soft. Add the peas, asparagus, and roasted tomatoes. Deglaze the pan with the white wine and add the lemon juice, mushroom stock, and fresh herbs. Remove all the ingredients from the pan and set aside. Using same pan, add the butter, stirring constantly until the sauce has completely liquefied. Remove from heat.

To serve, create the foundation of each stack on a plate with the mushroom mixture, then place a phyllo disk on top of the mixture, and then repeat the process. Top with the sauce. Bouchon traditionally stacks three layers, then garnishes the stack with shaved Pecorino Tartufo.

Cava Restaurant & Bar

1212 Coast Village Road, Montecito
(805) 969-8500
www.cavarestaurant.com
Owners: The Lopez-Hollis family

There's no shortage of Mexican- and Spanish-influenced cuisine in California, but on Coast Village Road in celebrity-studded Montecito, there's a friendly restaurant that's just about as famous as the neighborhood residents.

Accentuated with shimmering crystal, fresh floral arrangements, and vibrant terra cotta walls, Cava Restaurant & Bar is where to go if you're craving authentic Latin cuisine from South America, Spain, and Mexico served in a fun, relaxing atmosphere. And if you time it right, you can enjoy your food while listening to live Spanish guitar.

Homemade tamales, grilled Anaheim chile rellenos, rock shrimp soft tacos . . . Cava's menu is long and extravagant. Frequent visitors like to boast about the fresh chips served with two exciting salsas and the guacamole homemade with California avocados. And the cocktails are equally impressive. Belly up to the bar for a fresh blood-orange margarita, a Brazilian caipirinha, a Picasso, or a Barcelona. Hungry and can't wait 'til

lunch or dinner? No problem. Drop into Cava and grab a comfortable booth for an early morning breakfast, and feast on classics like huevos rancheros or the hearty and bold Grilled Churrasco Ribeye Steak and Eggs Piquante.

Because the weather is always nice here, request a table on the patio to enjoy the California sunshine. In the evenings, it tends to get chilly, but Cava has plenty of heat lamps to keep you warm—should you find that the cocktails and spices don't fully do the trick.

Gambas al Ajillo

These hot and spicy garlic shrimp are a delicious seafood small plate, and they're wonderful served with crusty slices of baguette and a Spanish white wine.

SERVES 4

½ cup olive oil

Fresh extra-large shrimp (8/10 count), peeled and deveined

6 garlic cloves, chopped

¼ cup Spanish white wine (Albariño)

¼ teaspoon crushed red pepper flakes

Coarse salt, to taste

In a heavy 7-inch skillet over medium-high heat, combine the olive oil, shrimp, and garlic. Add the wine, red pepper flakes, and salt. Cook for about 3 minutes, or until shrimp are just cooked.

Transfer to small casserole dish while the shrimp are still hot and serve immediately with sliced baguette.

CELEBRITY-STUDDED MONTECITO

Just east of Santa Barbara, tucked into the lower foothills of the Santa Ynez Mountains, sits the quietly posh town of Montecito. Claiming one of the wealthiest zip codes in the country, Montecito is home to celebrities, business titans, well-heeled regular folks, and on a part-time basis, Oprah.

With a population hovering around 10,000 in about nine square miles, the tiny high-end hamlet bustles with genteel activity in its two commercial sections, Coast Village Road and the Upper Village. You might just spot a celeb or two prowling the tony boutiques and shops, restaurants, and art galleries that dot the tree-lined streets.

Behind the well-manicured hedges, along winding, shaded lanes, are elegant estates, many of which were built at the turn of the last century by wealthy Easterners. Luxe lodgings include the Spanish-Colonial Four Seasons Resort, the Biltmore Santa Barbara, built in 1927, and the historic San Ysidro Ranch, both owned by Beanie Baby mogul Ty Warner. Each hotel has been host to a slew of Hollywood weddings; the Ranch was a honeymoon haven for the likes of Jack and Jackie Kennedy and Julia Roberts and husband Danny Moder.

TORTILLA ESPAÑOLA

Tortilla española is Spain's national dish. A favorite of tapas bars and eaten at all times of the day, this delicious tortilla can be made in advance (and even tastes better that way).

SERVES 6

1 cup olive oil
4–6 potatoes (about 1 pound), cut into
  ½-inch cubes
1 large onion, peeled and thinly sliced
6 eggs
Coarse salt and freshly ground black pepper,
  to taste
½ cup chopped fresh parsley, for garnish

In a deep, heavy 9-inch skillet over medium-high heat, combine the olive oil, potatoes, and onion. Sauté for 1–2 minutes, and then reduce the temperature. Cook for about 10 minutes, or until potatoes are tender. Remove the potatoes and onion from the skillet and drain on paper towels. Reserve the oil and set aside.

Preheat the oven to 350°F.

In a bowl, combine the eggs and salt and pepper, and beat with a fork for about 3 minutes. Add the cooked potatoes and onion to the egg mixture.

Heat 2 tablespoons of the reserved oil in the skillet over medium heat, until smoking. Pour in the potato and egg mixture and spread evenly in the skillet. Cook for about 1 minute, shaking the skillet often to avoid sticking. Reduce the heat and continue cooking until the eggs are brown underneath and the top is nearly firm.

Place a plate on top of the skillet and flip the omelet onto the plate. Add more oil to the skillet and slide the omelet back in, "uncooked" side down. Quickly transfer the skillet to the oven. Bake for approximately 5 minutes, until cooked evenly.

Transfer the omelet to a plate and let stand until cool. Sprinkle with parsley and serve cut into wedges.

Downey's

1305 State Street, Santa Barbara
(805) 966-5006
www.downeyssb.com
Owners: John and Liz Downey

If you're looking for a small, cozy restaurant where the owner is not only the chef, but also a steward of the environment when it comes to serving consistently good organic fruits and vegetables, sustainable seafood, and naturally raised beef and poultry, visit Downey's Restaurant on State Street.

Since 1982, chef-owner John Downey and his wife Liz (who'll greet you at the door) have been serving seasonal, nutritious dishes to those who appreciate good food. Surrounded by original art (much of which Liz has painted herself), mismatched furniture, and estate-like touches, guests will feel cozy and comfortable as they peruse an impressive menu that changes daily. That's because John scours the neighborhood markets every morning for the freshest of ingredients, hand-selecting only those items that meet his high quality and environmental standards.

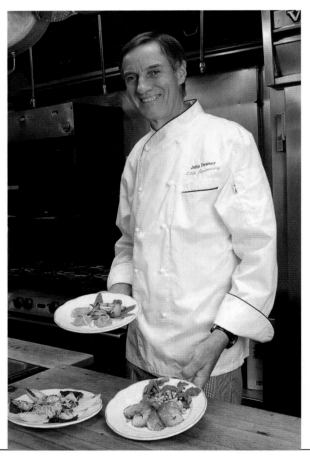

John created the Shell Bean Ragout featured here for the very first Harvest Moon Dinner at Tom Shepherd's Farm. It is simple enough to prepare but relies on the best possible ingredients. Downey originally used a mixture of four types of freshly harvested shell beans, though this recipe calls for only one. The choice is yours.

Lobster Flan, also featured here, is a perennial holiday favorite for the Downeys. It's simple to prepare and will definitely impress your guests. It can be made using either Maine lobster or California spiny lobster (when in season).

Harvest Moon Shell Bean Ragout

For the semi-dried tomatoes, start with fresh tomatoes like "Early Girl." Cut them in quarters and season with black pepper and garlic salt. Place the tomatoes on a rack, like a cooling rack, and dry them in a very low oven for several hours.

SERVES 6

1 cup fresh shell beans, cleaned

½ small onion, 3 cloves of garlic, and assorted herbs in a cheesecloth bag

1 tablespoon olive oil

2 tablespoons chopped fresh herbs (basil, oregano, rosemary, sage, thyme)

Salt and freshly ground black pepper, to taste

1 tablespoon butter

½ small onion, cut into large dice

2 cups vegetable stock (or chicken stock)

¼ cup heavy cream

½ cup semi-dried tomatoes (if substituting fully dried tomatoes, soak them in a little warm water for 1 hour prior to use)

2 ripe avocados, peeled, pitted, diced, and tossed with a squeeze of lemon juice

Add the fresh shell beans to a pot of fresh cold water. Do not add any salt at this point. Add the bag of aromatics and bring to a boil over high heat. Reduce the heat and simmer until beans are tender, about 1 hour for fresh beans. When the beans are cooked, drain well and transfer them to a bowl. Discard the aromatics.

Add the olive oil, freshly chopped herbs, and salt and pepper to the bowl of beans. Toss well and set aside.

Melt the butter in a medium saucepan over medium heat. Add the onion and sauté until it starts to brown slightly. Add the beans and vegetable stock. Bring to a boil. Add the heavy cream and remove from the heat. Check the seasoning and adjust if necessary.

Warm six soup bowls, and divide the dried tomatoes and avocado pieces between them. Spoon the beans and stock over them and serve.

LOBSTER FLAN

To add an elegant touch to this dish, try adding a slice of fresh truffle to each cup prior to baking.

SERVES 6–12

3 cups cream, plus more as needed

1 cup water

2 ounces cooked lobster meat, minced
   (a 1¼-pound lobster should yield 2 ounces
   with some left over; save the shell)

6 large eggs

Salt and white pepper, to taste

Pinch of nutmeg

Pinch of cayenne pepper

1 tablespoon cognac

In a stockpot over low heat, gently simmer the cream, water, and coarsely chopped lobster shell for about 30 minutes. Strain, pressing all the liquid through. If the liquid yields less than 1 quart, make up the difference by adding more cream.

Preheat the oven to 350°F.

In a mixing bowl, beat the eggs, and add the salt and pepper, nutmeg, and cayenne. Mix well, being careful not to incorporate too much air. Add the cognac and hot cream mixture, stirring quickly.

Divide the lobster meat among six 3½-ounce soufflé cups. Pour the flan mixture over. Place the cups in a shallow pan and place in oven. Carefully add water to the pan until covering the cups half way (this helps the cooking process by providing gentle heat around the cups). Bake until just set, about 40 minutes.

Serve flan warm with thin slices of toasted French bread.

EMILIO'S RISTORANTE & BAR

324 WEST CABRILLO BOULEVARD, SANTA BARBARA
(805) 966-4426
WWW.EMILIOSRESTAURANT.COM
OWNER: MICHAEL DEPAOLA

With Santa Barbara heralded as the "American Riviera," it's only fitting that the seaside community include Mediterranean-inspired restaurants. One of the most elegant and affordable of these is Emilio's Ristorante & Bar.

Emilio's, named after proprietor Michael DePaola's father, who helped his son build the restaurant after a fire destroyed their initial dream of a pizzeria, is a permanent fixture of the Santa Barbara dining scene. "Our mission," adds general manager Tom Dolan, "is to nurture the brand and to continue Emilio's tradition of offering an exceptional dining experience in a comfortable atmosphere."

Through the years, locals and visitors from around the world have made Emilio's an international success. A key contributor to that success has been the restaurant's ability to offer consistent quality in a charming-yet-unpretentious environment, combined with Emilio's enviable location on Santa Barbara's picturesque beachfront. This was the original vision for Emilio's, a vision that continues today.

If you've never visited Emilio's, you're in for a real treat. Amidst the smooth jazz, fragrant flowers, and candlelit tables is an extraordinarily creative menu that includes such favorites as Rock Shrimp Gnocchi, Braised Beef and Pork Ragu Lasagna, a heavily seafood-laden cioppino, and fresh local sea bass. The bar, Bar de Isabella, offers great half-price appetizers, including garlic fries and sesame cones stuffed with fresh ahi tuna, as well as DePaola's estate wines from his vineyards. Late afternoon on Thursday and Friday, celebrate "Indulgence Hour" at Emilio's: Besides sipping DePaola's wonderful wines, be sure to order an Isabellatini or the restaurant's twist on the Moulin Rouge.

PAELLA

SERVES 6–8

2 cups prepared saffron rice

4–7 precooked chicken thighs

4 ounces precooked sweet Italian sausage

1 cup fresh fish pieces (salmon, halibut, cod, etc.)

16 medium shrimp (16/20 count), peeled and deveined

16 Manila clams

16 mussels

1½ cups fish stock

½ cup tomato sauce

1 pinch crushed red pepper flakes

1 pinch oregano

1 teaspoon fresh garlic, peeled and minced

½ tablespoon extra-virgin olive oil

Salt and freshly ground black pepper, to taste

1 tablespoon green peas

Preheat the oven to 375°F.

In the bottom of a wide, shallow pan, preferably a paella pan, layer the rice, followed by the chicken, sausage, fish pieces, shrimp, clams, and mussels. Pour the fish stock and tomato sauce over the top, followed by the red pepper flakes, oregano, garlic, olive oil, and salt and pepper.

Place pan in the oven and roast until the clams and mussels start to open, about 8 to 10 minutes. At this point, toss and mix the ingredients together every few minutes to coat them and keep the ingredients moist. (This is best done using an oven mitt and heavy wooden spoon.) When all of the clams and mussels have opened (discard any unopened shellfish), add the peas, and check the seasoning and adjust if necessary.

Transfer paella to small plates or bowls to serve.

GOAT CHEESE & GORGONZOLA CROSTADA

SERVES 4–6

4 ounces Gorgonzola

4 ounces goat cheese

1 package shredded phyllo (puff pastry)

2 tablespoons olive oil

Caramelized walnuts and pears:

1 semi-ripe Bartlett pear, peeled, seeded,
    and cut into ½-inch cubes

½ cup walnuts, toasted in a 350°F oven for
    10 minutes

¼ cup sugar

1 tablespoon butter

1 tablespoon balsamic vinegar

Shallot dressing:

2 tablespoons fresh lemon juice

¼ cup balsamic vinegar

1 teaspoon chopped fresh thyme

1 teaspoon kosher salt

1 teaspoon freshly ground black pepper

1 garlic clove

1 whole shallot, peeled

1 cup extra-virgin olive oil

4 ounces mixed young lettuces

Let the Gorgonzola and goat cheese stand at room temperature for 30 minutes to soften.

In the bowl of a stand mixer, combine the Gorgonzola and goat cheese. Mix on medium speed until completely combined. Scoop the cheese into balls with a 1-ounce ice-cream scoop.

Defrost the shredded phyllo (if frozen) and lightly fluff it apart. Carefully encase the cheese balls with the phyllo, pressing the dough tightly around the cheese. When all the cheese balls are wrapped in dough, press each ball flat, forming a thick coin shape.

Heat olive oil in a nonstick pan. Once hot, add the crostadas and brown on both sides. Remove from heat and hold in a warm oven until ready to serve.

To make the caramelized walnuts and pears, heat a large sauté pan over high heat. Add the pears and do not touch them for 1–2 minutes. Once the pears are browning, you can loosen them. Continue browning pears until they are evenly browned.

Grind the toasted walnuts in a food processor until they're half their original size. Add them to the pan with the pears and continue cooking for at least 3 minutes. Add the sugar and caramelize by allowing the sugar to melt and cook until it browns. Add the butter and vinegar and cook until you have a saucy mixture. Remove from heat and pour mixture onto a sheet pan to cool.

To make the shallot dressing, combine the lemon juice, vinegar, thyme, salt, pepper, garlic, and shallot in a blender. Blend until combined. With the blender running, slowly add the oil and blend until dressing is emulsified.

To serve, toss the lettuces with the vinaigrette and place on the center of small plates. Top with the caramelized nuts and pears, and top again with a warm crostada or two.

THE HITCHING POST II

406 EAST HIGHWAY 246, BUELLTON
(805) 688-0676
WWW.HITCHINGPOST2.COM
OWNER: FRANK OSTINI

Just off Highway 101 in Buellton (forty minutes north of Santa Barbara), a legendary restaurant famous for its Santa Maria barbecue and exceptional central California wines awaits your dining pleasure (just look for the yellow sign out front—you can't miss it).

Featured in the Academy Award–winning film *Sideways,* the Hitching Post II is where you go if you're after big, juicy barbecued steaks, baby back ribs, grilled seafood, and the restaurant's private label wine (order the Pinot Noir). Be sure to call ahead for a reservation, because this fun, unpretentious steakhouse gets packed—usually from a combination of local ranchers and tourists vacationing for the weekend. Inside is a lively atmosphere amidst old-school decor: wood paneling and checkered tablecloths give this restaurant rustic charm.

While charming, the decor isn't the main attraction. Instead, patrons come to feast on the open-fire-cooked, oak-infused food. For starters, the "magic dusted" fries and garlic bread are must-haves, as are the large artichokes prepared on the grill—by far the most popular appetizer (and featured here). If you're a carnivore, it's hard to choose between the sizable and perfectly charred fillet, New York strip, Angus rib chop, or top sirloin. This isn't the place for vegetarians, but if you aren't tempted by the succulent Gulf shrimp, Texas quail, or the California rack of lamb, order the incredibly authentic stuffed pasilla peppers (also featured here), the barbecue mushrooms, or the fresh vegetable trays. No matter what you choose, the food and wine are both traditional and delicious.

GRILLED PASILLA PEPPER STUFFED WITH PRAWN & PROVOLONE

Make grilled corn salsa according to the following recipe, Smoked Duck & Grilled Corn Quesadillas.

SERVES 4

4 large prawns (such as spot prawns)
4 tablespoons butter, melted
¼ cup white wine
¼ cup lemon juice
4 pasilla chiles
8 slices (1 ounce each) provolone cheese

Remove the shells from the spot prawns, devein, and rise under cold water. Pat dry and skewer the prawns on a bamboo or metal skewer.

Next, in a large bowl or deep pan, combine the butter, white wine, and lemon juice, reserving some of the marinade for marinating the peppers. Mix well. Add the skewered prawns and allow to marinate for at least 15 minutes. While the prawns are marinating, heat an outdoor grill or barbecue. When hot, grill the marinated prawns for 2–3 minutes per side, or until just opaque. Remove from heat and set aside.

On the same grill or barbecue, grill the peppers. Allow the pepper skin to burn to black char. Remove from heat and cover the peppers for 15 minutes to cool. When cool, peel and discard the burnt skin. Slit open each pepper and remove the seeds and inside rib fibers (that's where all the heat is). Be careful not to tear the peppers.

Slice the prawns lengthwise. Place 1 or 2 slices of cheese and a half or whole prawn (depending on size) inside the cavity of each pepper. Marinate the peppers for 15 minutes in the butter/lemon mixture. Return the peppers to the grill and cook until the cheese is melted.

Serve with a side of grilled corn salsa.

BUELLTON

Known as the Gateway to the Santa Ynez Valley, Buellton is tucked in at the intersection of Highway 101 and CA 246, about 40 miles from Santa Barbara. It's also known as the Home of the Original Split Pea Soup, thanks to the hordes of hungry travelers from all over the world who have flocked to Pea Soup Andersen's restaurant for sustenance and hospitality for more than 85 years.

The town gets its name from Vermont-born Rufus Thompson Buell, who settled in the area after buying, along with his brother, a quarter of the 26,000-acre Rancho San Carlos de Jonata, a Mexican land grant. By 1872 R. T. Buell had bought the entire rancho and dissolved the partnership with his brother. While the Buell property prospered as a horse and cattle ranch and dairy farm, stores and businesses popped up on the main street.

Today's Buellton continues to thrive, with full-service hotels, motels, inns, wine-tasting rooms, shops, and restaurants. One of the town's best-known restaurants is the Hitching Post II, which has won rave reviews since 1986 for its slow oak-grilled meats and its addictive French fries, named the best in Southern California by the *Los Angeles Times*. The restaurant and bar had a turn in the Hollywood spotlight in the Academy Award–winning movie *Sideways*.

Smoked Duck & Grilled Corn Quesadillas

MAKES 4 QUESADILLAS

Dressing:

¼ bunch fresh cilantro, stems removed
2 tablespoons olive oil
2 tablespoons white wine vinegar
2 tablespoons lime juice
¼ jalapeño, seeded and chopped
1 garlic clove
1 tablespoon chopped green onion
Salt and freshly ground black pepper, to taste

Grilled corn salsa:

2 ears of corn, husked
Melted butter, as needed
Lemon juice, as needed
Salt and freshly ground black pepper, to taste
1 teaspoon minced fresh ginger
¼ red onion, diced
Olive oil, as needed, to saute
½ red bell pepper, diced

Cilantro lime cream:

½ cup sour cream
2 tablespoons minced fresh cilantro
2 tablespoons lime juice
1 teaspoon tequila

Quesadillas:

1 duck breast, skin-on
Melted butter, as needed
Lemon juice, as needed
Salt and freshly ground black pepper, to taste
4 flour tortillas
1 cup Jack cheese
Butter, as needed

To make the dressing: Combine the cilantro, olive oil, vinegar, lime juice, jalapeño, garlic, green onion, and salt and pepper in a blender or food processor. Blend until smooth. Set aside.

To make the grilled corn salsa: Baste the corn with melted butter and lemon juice. Season with salt and pepper and place on a hot outdoor grill or barbecue. Turn occasionally, to ensure even cooking, and remove from heat before the corn is fully cooked. When cool to the touch, remove the kernels from the cobs.

Next, in a sauté pan over medium heat, sauté the ginger and red onions with a little olive oil for 3 minutes. Add the red pepper and corn kernels. Cook for 2 minutes or until warm. Remove from heat and add the dressing. Mix well and keep warm.

To make the cilantro lime cream: Combine the sour cream, cilantro, lime juice, and tequila in a blender. Puree until smooth.

Baste the duck breast with butter and lemon and season with salt and pepper (like you did with the corn). Place on a hot outdoor grill or barbecue, skin-side down, to crisp the skin. Remove the duck while it's still pink in the center, about 8 to 10 minutes. Dice the meat when cool.

To assemble: Lay tortillas on a flat work surface. Place 2 tablespoons of each ingredient on one half of each tortilla: first the cheese, then corn salsa, duck, and 2 more tablespoons of cheese on top. Fold each tortilla in half and butter both sides. Place on the hot outdoor grill or barbecue and grill until crispy and warmed through, about 1 or 2 minutes. Cut quesadillas into quarters and serve each with a dollop of the cilantro lime cream.

TRI-TIP AND SANTA MARIA–STYLE BARBECUE

If you haven't spent time on the Central Coast of California, chances are you haven't heard of tri-tip. A cut of beef that sits at the bottom of the sirloin, tri-tip (also known as triangle roast) is small and, yes, triangular, usually weighing 1½ to 2½ pounds.

The cut was primarily used for ground beef or sliced into steaks or cubes until the late 1950s, when it began to be marketed on its own. Soon it became a local specialty in Santa Maria, where it remains a must-have at barbecues. The traditional Santa Maria style of cooking traces its roots to the area's old rancho days. The meat is barbecued at low heat over a red oak pit (the wood is native to the region), but tri-tip can also be slow-smoked, marinated, or seasoned with a dry rub and cooked over high heat on a grill, on a rotisserie, or in an oven.

After cooking, the meat is sliced across the grain and often served with pinquito beans (small pink beans grown in the Santa Maria Valley; small red or pinto beans make a good substitute), salsa, green salad, French bread, and a local red wine. Santa Maria claims tri-tip as its own, but the mouthwatering meat has become a sure-fire hit far and wide for its wallet-friendly versatility, lower fat content, and flavor.

GRILLED ARTICHOKES WITH
SPICY SMOKED TOMATO MAYONNAISE

SERVES 6

6 artichokes

Mayonnaise (yields approximately 1½ quarts):

4 ounces garlic cloves
1 pound onions large, sliced thin
4 pasilla chiles, halved
4 tomatoes, halved
1 teaspoon cayenne pepper
1 teaspoon chili powder
1 teaspoon paprika
1 teaspoon salt
1 quart mayonnaise

2 tablespoons butter, melted
2 tablespoons olive oil
2 tablespoons white wine
2 tablespoons lemon juice
Salt and fresh ground black pepper, for seasoning

Break off the artichokes' small outside leaves. Cut off the tops with a knife and remove the sharp points of the leaves with scissors. Soak the artichokes in water, and wash with cold water to remove any sand. Place the artichokes into a vegetable steamer with the tips up. Cover and cook until the hearts are tender, approximately 25–35 minutes, depending upon the size of the artichokes. (To check the hearts, cut into the base of each artichoke to make sure it is soft and the inside leaves can be easily pulled out.) Cook 5 additional minutes if artichokes are not done, then check again, repeating as necessary. Remove artichokes from heat and drain upside down on paper towel, allowing the artichokes to cool. When cool, cut them in half and remove the fuzzy choke with a spoon.

To make the spicy smoked tomato mayonnaise, prepare an outdoor grill or barbecue for low heat. Slow roast the garlic cloves and onions until soft and the peppers and tomatoes until semisoft. Remove the vegetables from the heat and put them in a blender. Puree until smooth and transfer to a mixing bowl. Add the cayenne pepper, chili powder, paprika, and salt. Mix well. Fold in the mayonnaise and mix well. Set aside.

Make an artichoke marinade by combining in a bowl the melted butter, olive oil, white wine, lemon juice, and salt and pepper. Increase the outdoor grill or barbecue to high heat. Place the artichokes on the grill and baste with the marinade. Continue to grill until the artichokes are warm and crispy. Serve with the mayonnaise.

THE PALACE GRILL

8 EAST COTA STREET, SANTA BARBARA
(805) 963-5000
WWW.PALACEGRILL.COM
OWNERS: MICHAEL AND SANDY DEROUSSE

Tucked along a side road off downtown State Street is the Palace Grill. What makes this restaurant truly extraordinary is its unconventional approach to local fare. That's because this establishment doesn't serve California fare, but rather some of the finest New Orleans–style cuisine this side of the Mississippi.

It's Mardi Gras every day of the year at the Palace Grill. Because the establishment doesn't take reservations Friday and Saturday, patrons line up early for tables and dance and listen to live music outside the front doors as they wait. This neighborhood restaurant is first-come, first-served. Insider tip: If the line gets too long, complimentary appetizers are often passed up and down the sidewalk for the hungry—and patient—would-be diners.

From Cajun to Creole, this bayou-themed funhouse serves up all the popular favorites—jambalaya, crawfish etouffée, New Orleans–style barbecue shrimp, blackened filet mignon, Louisiana bread pudding soufflé, and colossal Cajun martinis in old-fashioned Mason jars. The restaurant is roomy, and has a large bar, so you'll find plenty of space to mingle and feast.

"As soon as you walk in, you can feel the energy and excitement, and the group sing-alongs are electrifying," say owners Michael and Sandy DeRousse. Every table in this eighty-seat restaurant is treated as if it is the only one—the service is that good. And if you are celebrating a birthday or special event, the Palace Grill will go the extra mile, including personalizing your plate with a message inked in chocolate.

Louisiana Barbecue Shrimp

These are the shrimp served in New Orleans's finer restaurants. The Palace Grill uses a modified recipe, adding beer and Worcestershire sauce and reducing the amount of butter. In New Orleans, shrimp are served whole, head and all, with a loaf of French bread.

SERVES 4

4 tablespoons butter

2 pounds medium shrimp (16/20 count), shells on (head-on works great, too)

2 teaspoons salt

1 teaspoon "three pepper" (one part each cayenne pepper, white pepper, and freshly ground black pepper)

2 tablespoons ground rosemary

3 tablespoons minced fresh garlic

1 cup Worcestershire sauce

1 cup beer

2 tablespoons fresh lemon juice

4 cups cooked white rice

In a large sauté pan over medium to high heat, combine the butter, shrimp, salt, three pepper, and rosemary. Sauté the shrimp on one side for approximately 2 minutes, or until the shells begin to turn color. Turn the shrimp over and add the garlic, Worcestershire sauce, beer, and lemon juice. Cook until the liquid is reduced by half. Serve shrimp and liquid immediately over white rice.

Jalapeño-Cheddar Corn Muffins

MAKES 2½ DOZEN

1 cup cornmeal
1½ cups plus 2 tablespoons all-purpose flour
2½ tablespoons baking powder
3 eggs
⅓ cup plus 1 tablespoon melted butter or margarine
¼ cup honey
⅓ cup vegetable shortening
1¾ cups milk
2 jalapeño peppers, finely diced
5 ounces cheddar cheese, finely grated

Preheat the oven to 350°F.

In a large mixing bowl, combine the cornmeal, flour, and baking powder. In a smaller bowl, combine the eggs, margarine, and honey. Mix well. Fold the shortening into the dry ingredients until crumbly. Then add the moist ingredients to the dry ingredients. Mix just until the dry ingredients are moistened. Add the milk. Mix well. Add the jalapeños and cheese. Mix again. Scoop the batter into lightly greased muffin tins.

Bake in the preheated oven for 10–15 minutes, or until golden brown. Serve warm.

CALIFORNIA CHILE PEPPERS

Chile peppers have long been the secret weapon in many types of cuisine, used to add zip and fiery flavor nuances in Africa, Southeast Asia, China, India, and much of North and South America. In the United States, chiles traditionally have been associated with Southwestern food, but they're catching on like wildfire in other parts of the country as well.

The Central Coast is one of four main California production areas for chile peppers. The majority are processed into salsas (got chips?) or canned whole. The remainder are sold fresh and range from relatively mild Anaheims to heat-packin' habañeros. A favorite Mexican dish, chile rellenos (stuffed chiles), is made with roasted fresh poblano pepper (you can substitute Hatch green chile, Anaheim, pasilla, or jalapeño).

Tips for cooking with chile peppers: Always taste them and the dish you are adding them to. In general, longer and thinner peppers tend to be hotter. You can cool the heat of a pepper by cutting it in half and removing the pithy ribs and seeds. When buying fresh chile peppers, look for tight, glossy skins and firm bruise-free peppers with no soft spots. Wear rubber gloves when working with them, being careful not to touch your eyes or face. Wash your hands thoroughly when finished.

PETROS LOS OLIVOS RESTAURANT

2860 GRAND AVENUE, LOS OLIVOS
(805) 686-5455
WWW.PETROSRESTAURANT.COM
OWNER: PETROS BENEKOS

On Grand Avenue in the heart of wine-studded Los Olivos (forty-five minutes north of Santa Barbara) is the lavish Fess Parker's Wine Country Inn. You remember Fess Parker? The actor who played Davy Crockett and Daniel Boone in the '50s and '60s? Before his passing in 2010, Fess built quite a winery (Fess Parker Winery and Vineyards) and resort in Santa Barbara County. Today, his legacy lives on; Petros, tucked inside the Inn, is honored to serve incredible cuisine to those who visit.

In a chic atmosphere with white walls, elegant wood floors, marble tabletops, and unpretentious class, Petros is a fusion of California and Greek cuisine. Serious foodies, you will be pleasantly surprised to find the menu is truly authentic—it does not feature anything that's been Americanized. "You won't find hummus in my restaurant, nor a 'Greek salad' with lettuce and vinaigrette," says chef Petros Benekos. "Those clichés are not true Greek cuisine." But what you will find on the daily menu are creatively prepared dishes like Horiatiki Salad with Volos Olives, Kafteri Chicken Pizza, classic moussaka, and Feta-Crusted Rack of Lamb.

You can enjoy Petros's fabulous cuisine either inside or outside on the lovely patio. The Petros Bar is a perfect and cozy place to kick back, nibble on some amazing appetizers, and unwind with one of Petros's signature Bloody Marys, a glass of Fess Parker Pinot Noir, or the local Firestone beer on tap. Don't be surprised if a few friendly wine tasters stumble in and join you. Remember, Grand Avenue is also home to tasting room after tasting room.

GRILLED MIXED VEGETABLES

SERVES: 6–8

1 medium onion
1 eggplant
2 zucchini
2 green bell peppers
2 yellow bell peppers
2 red bell peppers
1 cup olive oil
½ cup white vinegar
1 teaspoon dried oregano
Salt and freshly ground black pepper, to taste
¼ cup fresh lemon juice

Cut the onion, eggplant, zucchini, and all the peppers into 1-inch pieces.

Marinate the vegetables in a bowl with the olive oil, vinegar, oregano, and salt and pepper. Mix with your hands to combine. Let the vegetables marinate for 45 minutes to 1 hour.

Place the vegetables on a hot outdoor grill or barbecue for 4 or 5 minutes turning them to cook both sides. Remove from heat.

Place the vegetables on a serving platter and drizzle with fresh lemon juice.

LOS OLIVOS

This historic Western-style town of 1,000 souls in the Santa Ynez Valley has evolved into an upscale but low-key destination for art, wine, and food. Smack-dab in the center of wine country, surrounded by sage-green and golden rolling hills, expansive vineyards, and horse ranches, the cowboy-chic town is a must-visit—no spurs required.

The main drag, Grand Avenue, sports a flagpole (a World War I monument) at its center, and the town bustles around it, offering more than two dozen wine-tasting rooms and wine stores, art galleries, boutiques, an inn and spa, and dining spots from California casual to white-tablecloth elegant. A sense of history wafts through the air like a fine wine's bouquet. Many of the tasting rooms are housed in Victorian-style buildings, and an 1886 stagecoach stop houses a top-notch restaurant.

Following the area's transition from stagecoach to the Pacific Coast Railway, land auctions held in 1887 created the quaint village of Los Olivos ("the olive trees"), named after a nearby ranch encompassing 5,000 olive trees. In a nod to the town's past, Global Gardens, a unique food-tasting venue and shop, offers samples of its locally grown award-winning organic extra-virgin olive oil.

SKEWERED CHICKEN

SOUVLAKI

This is a classic Greek appetizer.

SERVES 6

1 cup olive oil
½ cup lemon juice
2 garlic cloves, crushed
4 chicken breasts, boneless and skinless,
    cut into 1-inch pieces
2 green bell peppers, cut into 1-inch pieces
2 yellow bell peppers, cut into 1-inch pieces
2 red bell peppers, cut into 1-inch pieces
12 cherry tomatoes

In a small bowl, combine the olive oil, lemon juice, and garlic. Stir well to combine.

Arrange the chicken in a large dish and pour the marinade over the chicken. Use your hands to incorporate. Cover and let sit for 1–1½ hours, stirring occasionally.

Divide the chicken, peppers, and tomatoes equally among six metal or bamboo skewers. Pour the marinade over the top for extra flavor and brush the skewers with more marinade before placing on a hot outdoor grill or barbecue. Grill for 20–25 minutes, or until chicken is cooked through. Squeeze some lemon juice over skewers if desired.

BABY CHEESE PIES
WITH MINT

TYROPITAKIA

MAKES 30–40 SMALL PIES

1 pound dry feta
1 cup fresh Parmesan, thinly shaved
2–3 teaspoons freshly ground black pepper
4 teaspoons very thinly sliced fresh mint
1 packet of phyllo (puff pastry) dough
Olive oil, as needed, for cooking

Put the feta in a bowl, and with a spoon, smash and press the feta to soften it. Add the Parmesan and mix with the feta. Add the pepper and the chopped mint, and combine with the cheeses.

On a flat counter, begin rolling out the phyllo dough. Divide the dough into 4 or 5 large strips.

Use a large spoon to scoop the cheese out of the bowl. Place large scoops on the dough. Fold the dough with filling inside to form small triangles.

Refrigerate the phyllo dough pieces for about 1 hour.

If you'd like to fry the pies, place them in a large shallow frying pan, in batches, with about ½-inch deep of olive oil. Turn the pies occasionally, frying until crispy and golden brown on both sides.

If you prefer to bake the pies, preheat the oven to 375°F. Brush the top of the pies with a little olive oil and arrange them on a greased sheet pan. Bake until crispy and golden brown.

Remove the pies from heat. If fried, drain the pies on paper towel. If baked, rest them on parchment or wax paper.

The pies are best served hot, but they can also be served cold or at room temperature.

Salads, Starters & Soups

Whether it's a lazy summer afternoon or a crisp winter evening in Santa Barbara, these salads, starters, and soups are the perfect beginnings to invigorate the palate and rejuvenate the soul year-round. The salads are crisp, inviting, and made with wonderfully fresh ingredients. The starters are perfect comfort foods. And the soups, simmered over a hot kitchen flame, are always served with a smile. All three of these easy courses can be prepared as a prelude to the main meal or served as a lunch or dinner special.

Bella Vista, located inside the opulent Biltmore Four Seasons, introduces a Chilled Cucumber Gazpacho, an excellent dish to serve at a beach luncheon or on a sun-dappled patio. And the Sage & Butter Roasted Potato Gnocchi is a perfect starter to excite your dinner guests. Cozy Blue Agave, on a side street off of bustling State Street, lures food lovers in with a Salmon Ceviche, while up north, off the winding Chumash Highway, the historic Cold Spring Tavern tempts drivers and motorcyclists with hearty bowls of Wild Game Black Bean Chili.

Louie's makes a grand appearance with garden-fresh Tomato Salad and ocean-fresh Shrimp & Scallop Cakes, while the famed Montecito Cafe surprises first-timers with a rich bowl of Carrot Sesame Soup followed by exquisite Goat Cheese Pancakes. Miró, nestled inside Santa Barbara's world-famous Bacara Resort & Spa, convinces visitors to escape the sun for a moment to sample the Chilled Avocado Soup. And while inside the resort, why not also sample the Cheese Gnocchi with Chanterelle Mushrooms, Serrano Ham, Pea Tendrils & Sweet Curry Espuma? Can you say delicious? Santa Barbara's notable Opal Restaurant & Bar, always a local favorite, brings the sea to you with two outstanding starters—a Warm Pesto Sautéed Bay Scallop Salad and a beautiful small dish layered with Black Pepper–Crusted Seared Ahi Tuna. Last, but certainly not least, the Stonehouse at San Ysidro Ranch—Santa Barbara's best kept secret, which has welcomed presidents, celebrities, and billionaire tycoons—concludes the chapter with a traditional Tortilla Soup and a small plate of Creamy Blue Cheese Polenta with Rosemary & Grilled Portobello Mushroom. Bon appétit.

BELLA VISTA

1260 CHANNEL DRIVE, SANTA BARBARA
(805) 969-2261
WWW.FOURSEASONS.COM/SANTABARBARA/DINING/
OWNERS: TY WARNER AND THE BILTMORE

An opulent hotel amidst a perfect central California setting, the Four Seasons' Biltmore is the perfect choice for Santa Barbara tourists or residents looking for a little time away from home. Overlooking exclusive Butterfly Beach in famed Montecito, this coveted resort is one lavish paradise when it comes to accommodations, spa treatments, and fine dining.

Tucked inside the Biltmore is the acclaimed Bella Vista, a deluxe-yet-relaxed restaurant that excels at offering sensational coastal cuisine to its beloved guests. Led by executive chef Alessandro Cartumini, Bella Vista features Italian-inspired dishes that can be appreciated at breakfast, lunch, and dinner. Choose between the prime window seats inside the Italian-themed restaurant or outside on the lovely patio, complete with heat lamps and sweeping postcard views. If you can't get enough of the great food, make a reservation to attend one of Chef Cartumini's popular buffets, particularly the Italian dinner buffet or the seafood buffet. Bella Vista's famed Champagne Sunday brunch attracts devoted followers from near and far. Aside from the traditional brunch fare, expect to find fresh oysters on the half shell, local lobster, caviar, and all-you-can-drink mimosas. As they say, "You get what you pay for," so if you're willing to hand over your credit card, this is the place to come for exceptional food accompanied by some of Santa Barbara's most sought-after views.

Sage & Butter Roasted Potato Gnocchi with Onion Soubise, Sweet Corn, Tarragon, San Joaquin Gold Cheese & Bloomsdale Spinach

SERVES 4–6

Gnocchi:

1 pound russet potatoes (3 to 4 potatoes)

1 cup all-purpose flour

2 egg yolks

Freshly grated nutmeg, to taste

Salt, to taste

Onion soubise:

1 tablespoon extra-virgin olive oil

1 medium onion, julienned

1 garlic clove, chopped

1 fresh thyme sprig

2 tablespoons sherry

1 cup vegetable stock

Salt and freshly ground black pepper, to taste

4 tablespoons butter

8 medium sage leaves

1 ear of corn, shucked, grilled on each side,
     kernels removed with a sharp knife

1 handful roughly julienned spinach (Bloomsdale)

1 small handful tarragon leaves

2 ounces San Joaquin Gold Cheese
     (from California's Central Valley)

Bake the potatoes in a preheated 375°F oven until soft, about 1 hour. Remove from the oven and, when cool to the touch, remove the skins. Pass the potatoes through a potato ricer. Let the potatoes cool to room temperature. In a large mixing bowl, combine the mashed potatoes with the flour and egg yolks. Season with nutmeg and salt. Mix well without overworking.

When a "dough" is achieved, remove it from the bowl, and, on a floured work surface, cut the dough into ½-inch slices, and then into ½-inch sections. Dust the pieces with flour and roll them into cylinders. Next, cut the cylinders into ⅓-inch-long gnocchi. Cook the gnocchi in boiling salted water until they float. Drain and set aside.

To make the onion soubise: Heat the olive oil in a saucepan over low heat. Add the onion, garlic, and thyme. Cook until onion and garlic are very soft. Add the sherry and let reduce until dry. Add the vegetable stock and bring to a simmer. Cook 10 additional minutes, then remove the thyme sprig and blend the soubise in a kitchen blender until well emulsified. Season to taste with salt and pepper and set aside.

To assemble the dish: Heat a sauté pan over medium heat. Add the butter and sage, and sauté until browned. Add the cooked gnocchi and corn, and continue to sauté until the gnocchi are well coated with butter. Toss in the spinach and tarragon leaves and remove from heat. Spoon the soubise over serving dishes, and top with the gnocchi, corn, and spinach mixture. Shave the aged cheese over the top and serve immediately.

CHILLED CUCUMBER GAZPACHO WITH ALMOND PANNA COTTA & LIGURIAN OIL

SERVES 4

Gazpacho:

1 tablespoon extra-virgin olive oil (Ligurian)
2 tablespoons chopped shallot
1 cup peeled, seeded, and diced cucumber
1 pinch fresh mint leaves
1 pinch fresh dill
1¼ cups vegetable stock
1 cup sour cream
1 teaspoon lemon zest
Grated nutmeg, to taste

Panna cotta:

½ cup half-and-half
3 star anise
1 cinnamon stick
5 juniper berries
2 gelatin leaves (or 1 teaspoon powdered gelatin),
    steeped in cold water
Salt and freshly ground black pepper, to taste
1 tablespoon shaved toasted almonds

Garnish:

Thinly shaved cucumber ribbons from
    one-third cucumber
Sea salt, to taste
2 tablespoons extra-virgin olive oil (Ligurian)

To make the gazpacho: Heat the olive oil in a sauté pan over medium heat. Add the shallot and cook until soft. In a blender, combine the cooked shallots, cucumber, mint, dill, vegetable stock, sour cream, lemon zest, and nutmeg. Blend until well emulsified. Place in refrigerator to chill.

To make the panna cotta: Heat the half-and-half in a saucepan over low heat. Add the star anise, cinnamon, and juniper berries. Remove from heat, add the gelatin leaves, and season with salt and pepper. Whisk mixture well and strain out the solids. Add the almonds. Pour panna cotta into four individual molds like a ramekin or custard cup, and let set in the refrigerator until chilled.

To serve: Place one panna cotta in the middle of each serving bowl. Pour the gazpacho around the panna cotta. Top with cucumber ribbons. Sprinkle with sea salt and drizzle with olive oil.

BLUE AGAVE

20 EAST COTA STREET, SANTA BARBARA
(805) 899-4694
WWW.BLUEAGAVESB.COM
OWNER: GABI BARYSCH-CROSBIE

If your taste is for a dark and seductive restaurant with remarkable food, cozy tables next to a crackling fireplace, and comfortable booths in which to dine and sip a vintage Port after dinner, drop into Blue Agave off State Street in downtown Santa Barbara.

Named after the celebrated tequila plant, Blue Agave, which opened its doors in 1995, features live music, innovative cocktails, and a happy hour with fun menu items like "Grown Up" Grilled Cheese and Prickly Pear Margaritas, along with phenomenal cuisine in an informal-yet-romantic atmosphere.

"Blue Agave brings people together to eat, have a wonderful drink, and to converse," says proprietor Gabi Barysch-Crosbie. "We want you to come here to relax and kick back."

And kick back is what guests like to do at Blue Agave. After finishing their chicken mole enchiladas or Ligurian fish stew, many shift to the expansive bar to sample one of more than fifty boutique tequilas, while others head upstairs, drink in hand, to unwind on one of the plush sofas beside the fireplace. At this intimate restaurant, the staff will always treat you like a friend.

SALMON CEVICHE

SERVES 6

2 pounds fresh wild salmon, skin and bones removed

2 cups fresh lemon juice

3 whole tomatoes

¼ red onion

¼ bunch fresh cilantro

1 teaspoon diced jalapeño

1 teaspoon dried oregano

2 tablespoons extra-virgin olive oil

1 tablespoon fresh lime juice

1 tablespoon fresh orange juice

Salt and freshly ground black pepper, to taste

Corn tortilla chips, for garnish

Avocado slices, for garnish

Cut the salmon into ½-inch pieces. Pour the fresh lemon juice in a bowl, add the salmon, and let sit for 30 minutes.

Dice the tomatoes, onion, and cilantro very fine. Add to the bowl, along with the jalapeño, oregano, olive oil, lime juice, orange juice, and salt and pepper to taste. Mix well to combine.

Serve in a martini glass, preferably with corn tortilla chips. Garnish with avocado.

TY WARNER

Ty Warner is a well-recognized name in Santa Barbara. That's because the billionaire has gobbled up many of the lavish properties in town, including the Biltmore Four Seasons Resort, the San Ysidro Ranch in Montecito, and the Montecito Country Club. He even built an aquarium (the Ty Warner Sea Center) at the end of the Santa Barbara pier. For those not in the know, Warner is the toy manufacturer behind the Beanie Babies craze of the nineties. Today, he's counted among the wealthiest people in the world. He also raises and donates millions every year for notable charities such as the Andre Agassi Foundation for underprivileged children in Las Vegas, the Elizabeth Glaser Pediatric AIDS Foundation, and the American Red Cross, and he donates Beanie Babies for children in the Middle East.

Cold Spring Tavern

5995 Stagecoach Road, Santa Barbara
(805) 967-0066
www.coldspringtavern.com
Owners: Wayne and Joy Ovington Wilson

Cold Spring Tavern's first customers arrived aboard dusty stagecoaches hauling Wells Fargo money, boxes, mail, and passengers over the craggy steps of San Marcos Pass in the 1870s and 1880s. And it wasn't just the roads that were tough. The twists and turns among the trees at Cold Spring Canyon were the perfect setting for highway robberies. Despite the perils, travelers kept coming to Cold Spring Tavern—depending on it for a secure resting place and some of the most delicious meals the West had to offer.

Today, guests arrive by car or Harley-Davidson, and Cold Spring Tavern remains a haven for hungry travelers. The old and weathered establishment, virtually unchanged since the days of the stagecoach run, is rich in California history and old-time hospitality.

At Cold Spring Tavern, you can get a hearty home-style breakfast, great steaks, and fresh chicken and seafood, but it's the Old West menu that has earned Cold Spring Tavern its legendary status. Don't be surprised to find wild boar loin, homemade venison sausage, charbroiled buffalo burgers, stuffed pheasant breast, and sautéed elk and rabbit among the weekly specials. Another savory backcountry dining experience is the tavern's famous Wild Game Black Bean Chili (featured here).

Next time you're in the area, make it a point to visit this historic establishment. If you happen to be here on Sunday, you'll be greeted by live music and the best tri-tip sandwiches in Santa Barbara—bar none. Because of limited parking, you may find yourself walking a considerable distance, but it's well worth the effort. The best tactic is to arrive by motorcycle. You'll immediately connect with the throng of bikers.

Wild Game Black Bean Chili

MAKES ABOUT 1 GALLON

1½ pounds dry black beans

2½ pounds wild meat (venison, buffalo, or rabbit is recommended), chopped or ground to desired size

1½ pounds yellow onions, peeled and diced

1½ pounds fresh pasilla chiles, stemmed, seeded and diced

Canola oil, as needed

12 ounces diced tomatoes

2 tablespoons chili powder

1 tablespoon cumin seed

Salt and freshly ground black pepper, to taste

Sour cream, for garnish

Cheese (cheddar, jack, or Mexican blend), for garnish

Jalapeños, chopped, for garnish

Bay leaves, for garnish

In a large pot of boiling water, cook the black beans according to package directions. The amount of water left after cooking the beans will dictate the thickness of the chili; feel free to add water to yield your preferred chili consistency. Once the beans are tender, remove the pot from the heat and set aside.

In a large frying pan over medium-high heat, sauté the meat until browned. Remove the meat (leaving the fat in the pan) and set aside.

Add the onions and chiles to the hot pan, reduce heat to medium, and sauté until the onions are translucent. Use a little canola oil if the fat from the meat is insufficient.

Add the cooked meat, onions, and chiles to the bean pot. Add the diced tomatoes, along with the chili powder, cumin, and salt and pepper, to taste. Mix well, return the pot to the stove over low heat, cover, and let simmer for about 1 hour.

To serve, ladle the chili into soup bowls and place a dollop of sour cream, a sprinkling of cheese, and chopped jalapeños on top. Garnish with a bay leaf. Serve with crusty French or sourdough bread.

LOUIE'S CALIFORNIA BISTRO

1404 DE LA VINA STREET, SANTA BARBARA
(805) 963-7003
WWW.LOUIESSB.COM
OWNERS: ANN RIZZOLI AND TREY BROOKS

Dining at Louie's California Bistro, located inside the historic and quaint Upham Hotel, is much like dining in someone's beautiful backyard. Beneath a lush canopy of palm trees on De La Vina Street lies a sprawling Victorian-style porch accented with large Adirondack chairs and bordered by vibrant flower gardens. It is here where many guests come to unwind with a glass of fine wine while being greeted by ever-pleasant restaurant owners Ann Rizzoli and Trey Brooks.

"For those dining with us, they can enjoy a delicious and elegant meal either at the handsomely designed bar, at a peaceful candlelit table inside the restaurant, or outside on the heated veranda," says Ann. "There's even seating at one of the lovely wrought-iron tables in the courtyard."

Relying on fresh, high-quality ingredients from neighboring farmers, ranchers, and fishermen, Louie's prides itself on serving exquisite home-cooked meals, such as traditional BLTs, linguine with fresh clams, grilled meat loaf, homemade quiche, and warm chocolate brownies. As one local puts it, this restaurant is the "perfect choice without a lot of fluff."

And because Santa Barbara County is supplied with many premium wines, there's no shortage of local varietals on the wine list. All pair nicely with the interesting comfort foods found on the menu.

TOMATO SALAD

SERVES 4

8 medium vine-ripened Roma tomatoes, sliced
1 bunch fresh basil, stemmed and julienned
½ red onion, thinly sliced
Roasted pine nuts, to taste
Gorgonzola cheese, to taste

Dressing:

1 cup balsamic vinegar
1 cup olive oil
Garlic salt, to taste
Freshly ground black pepper, to taste

To make the dressing: Combine the vinegar, olive oil, garlic salt, and pepper. Mix well to combine.

Divide the tomatoes (about 2 per serving) and layer on each plate. Top the tomatoes with some of the basil and red onion. Sprinkle the pine nuts and Gorgonzola over the tomato salad. Finish with a drizzle of the dressing and serve.

SHRIMP & SCALLOP CAKES

SERVES 4–8 (MAKES 16 CAKES)

Vinaigrette:

¼ cup rice wine vinegar

¼ cup fresh lemon juice

1 cup good-quality olive oil

Sliced shallots, to taste

Green onions, chopped, to taste

Salt and freshly ground black pepper

12 ounces cooked fresh shrimp

6 ounces cooked fresh sea scallops

1 tablespoon finely diced red bell pepper

¼ cup Parmesan-flavored bread crumbs

1 tablespoon chopped fresh Italian parsley

Salt and freshly ground pepper, to taste

1 egg, beaten, if needed

1–2 tablespoons olive oil

Steamed asparagus (optional; about 3 spears
    per serving)

To make the vinaigrette: Combine the vinegar, lemon juice, olive oil, shallots, green onion, and salt and pepper in a mixing bowl. Whisk until well combined. Set aside.

In a food processor, finely chop the shrimp and scallops. Transfer to a mixing bowl, and add the bell pepper, bread crumbs, parsley, and salt and pepper. Form mixture into 1-ounce patties (you should be able to make about 16). The moisture from the shrimp and scallops should bind with the breadcrumbs; if the mixture is too dry, add a little beaten egg.

In a large sauté pan over medium-high heat, heat the olive oil. When hot, add the shrimp and scallop cakes, and sauté until golden brown on each side.

Plate the cakes and drizzle some vinaigrette over the top. Serve with a side of steamed asparagus (about 3 spears per serving).

LOS ALAMOS

The small, Western-style town of Los Alamos is nestled in the northern entry to the Santa Ynez Valley, just forty-five miles from Santa Barbara. Surrounded by picturesque vineyards and working ranches, it exudes an Old West rustic charm.

The town packs a lot into its seven-block-long main street, with a large antiques mall in the historic Pacific Coast Railway train depot, in addition to individual antiques shops, a unique cafe in an art gallery, a wine tasting room, and several restaurants. Locals and foodies from far and wide flock to Full of Life Flatbread for out-of-this-world all-natural flatbread pizza made almost exclusively from the produce of the local farmers' markets.

Los Alamos (Spanish for "the cottonwoods") is proud of its ranching heritage, and visitors can still watch roundups and cattle branding at the Price Ranch. The Union Hotel, built in the 1880s along the Wells Fargo stagecoach line, boasts a colorful and musical history: it played host to Johnny Cash, and Paul McCartney and Michael Jackson filmed the video "Say, Say, Say" in its Victorian-era rooms.

MONTECITO CAFE

1295 COAST VILLAGE ROAD, MONTECITO
(805) 969-3392
WWW.MONTECITOCAFE.COM
OWNERS: MARK AND MARGARET HUSTON

A sugar-white building on Coast Village Road is festively dressed with green plantation shutters, terra cotta tiles, and expansive windows rimmed with planter boxes and little white holiday lights. A large gurgling fountain inside is filled with radiant flowers, which are hand-picked daily. Welcome to the award-winning Montecito Cafe, a culinary oasis that will both delight and inspire.

Once home to Charlie Chaplin's Montecito Inn, this historic hotel now shares space with this charming cafe, thanks to husband and wife team Mark and Margaret Huston, who opened the Cafe in 1986 after graduating from the California Culinary Academy. Diners begin with a farm-fresh salad to set the stage for a California-infused lunch or dinner. If you really crave the greens, order one of the Cafe's sizable salad bowls. Most are tossed with some kind of savory protein—fresh Idaho trout, Dungeness crab, homemade lamb sausage, or sautéed chicken. The same can be said about the Cafe's signature pasta bowls. For dinner, try one of the popular grilled burgers or traditional entrees like a perfectly flamed filet mignon, New York steak, or leg of lamb. And don't forget dessert. The locals seem to prefer the coconut cake. For early risers, the Cafe also offers a classy breakfast amidst its tranquil Montecito setting. The Cafe welcomes walk-ins, so should you find yourself strolling along Coast Village Road one day, pop in for a delightful meal.

Carrot Sesame Soup

SERVES 4

4 tablespoons butter
1 pound carrots, peeled and roughly chopped
½ large onion, roughly chopped
All-purpose flour, as needed
2 quarts chicken stock
2 ounces fresh ginger, peeled
Toasted sesame seeds, for garnish
Sesame oil, for garnish
Salt and freshly ground black pepper, to taste

In a large sauté pan over medium-high heat, melt the butter. When melted, add the carrots and onions, and sauté until the onions are soft and translucent. Dust the carrots and onions with a little flour and add the chicken stock. Slowly bring to a boil, stirring occasionally. Add the ginger.

When the carrots are tender, remove pan from the heat. Separate the vegetables from the stock.

In a blender or food processor, puree the vegetables until smooth. Return the pureed vegetables to the stock and reheat the soup.

To serve, divide the soup among individual serving bowls and top with the toasted sesame seeds, a drizzle of sesame oil, and salt and pepper.

GOAT CHEESE PANCAKES

SERVES 4–6

6 eggs

1 cup all-purpose flour

½ teaspoon sugar

3 tablespoons sour cream, plus more for garnish

7 ounces goat cheese, crumbled

1 tablespoon butter, melted

Smoked salmon, thinly sliced

Golden caviar (also known as whitefish caviar),
    for garnish

In a mixing bowl, gently whip the eggs. Add the flour and sugar and mix to combine. Add the sour cream and goat cheese, and gently mix. Add the melted butter and stir gently until a pancake batter–like consistency is achieved. (If the mixture is too thick, add more sour cream. If the mixture is too thin, add more flour.)

Pour the batter on a nonstick griddle over medium heat to make individual pancakes. The cakes should be about 3 inches across. Cook, turning once, until golden brown on both sides.

Remove the cakes from the griddle and garnish with thinly sliced smoked salmon, sour cream, and golden caviar.

RED-TILE ROOFS

Santa Barbara is famous for its picture-postcard scenery, its ideal Mediterranean climate, and its distinctive architecture. Many buildings are graced with red-tile roofs, creamy stucco walls, arched entryways, wrought-iron gates, and colorful tilework. The city is a pleasing blend of Moorish, Spanish Revival, Spanish and Portuguese Colonial, Andalusian, and other Mediterranean styles of architecture, interspersed with beach bungalows, Cape Cod cottages, and Victorian grande dames.

The most visited landmark in the city, the Old Mission Santa Barbara, helped to set the architectural tone with its thick adobe walls, open courtyards, and red-tile roof. A turning point in the city's architectural evolution was the great earthquake that struck in 1925, prompting strict building codes and an architectural board of review to create a unified look. The city now keeps a low profile, with building heights limited to four stories.

One of the most photographed public buildings in the United States, the Santa Barbara County Courthouse was completed in 1929 and is an eye-popping example of Spanish-Moorish style. It's one stop on the popular self-guided Red-Tile Walking Tour, which includes adobes dating from the late 1700s through the 1800s, plus one of the first "shopping malls" in California, the 1924 El Paseo, with cobblestoned passageways, courtyards, and, you guessed it, a red-tile roof.

MIRÓ

8301 HOLLISTER AVENUE, GOLETA

(805) 571-4204

WWW.BACARARESORT.COM

OWNERS: THE BACARA RESORT & SPA

If you've ever vacationed or visited Santa Barbara before, there's a good chance you've heard, read about, or seen the ultra-lavish Bacara Resort & Spa off of famed Highway 101. This celebrity-studded retreat is where the actors, musicians, and industry moguls go to get away while enjoying seventy-eight acres of pristine beachfront as they're pampered to their heart's content. If you're dressed to the nines and looking for a gastronomic event, pull up to the Bacara valet, hand over the keys, and take a seat inside the resort's exclusive restaurant, named for the celebrated Spanish artist Joan Miró.

Given the opulent location, Miró is obviously not your everyday eatery. But if you desire that perfectly aged steak, a succulent lobster, or a plate of wonderfully textured foie gras, Miró will impress. The accompanying wine list is equally extraordinary, with more than 12,000 bottles in the restaurant cellar. Experienced sommeliers will assist you in selecting the perfect bottle to pair with your delicious meal, and the elite table service is always cordial and never forceful.

Extravagant dining does come with a cost, however, so unless money is no object, you might consider making a reservation when you have a special event to celebrate or are long overdue for a special evening out. Trust those who've dined at Miró—the experience will be well worth the dinner bill.

CHILLED AVOCADO SOUP

SERVES 6

3 ripe avocados (preferably ripe Hass)

1 garlic clove

1 shallot

¼ bunch fresh Italian parsley

Juice of 2 lemons

Pinch of cayenne pepper

2 cups low-fat milk

Salt and freshly ground black pepper, to taste

Cooked lobster or grilled shrimp, for garnish
   (optional)

Carefully run a kitchen knife around each avocado and separate the halves. Remove the pits and scoop out the avocado flesh with a spoon. Place the avocado flesh in a blender, and add the garlic, shallot, parsley, lemon juice, cayenne pepper, and milk. Blend until the mixture is smooth.

If the soup is a little thick, add a touch more milk. Season with salt and pepper and chill for at least 30 minutes before serving.

Serve soup alone or garnish with lobster or grilled shrimp.

Cheese Gnocchi with Chanterelle Mushrooms, Serrano Ham, Pea Tendrils & Sweet Curry Espuma

SERVES 6

2 egg yolks

1 pound Mató del Pirineu cheese (or farmer cheese or ricotta)

Pinch of ground nutmeg

¼ cup farina flour (or Cream of Wheat)

¼ cup semolina flour

⅓ cup panko bread crumbs

Salt and freshly ground black pepper, to taste

⅓ cup plus 2 tablespoons all-purpose flour

3 tablespoons olive oil, divided

6 tablespoons butter

3 ounces chanterelle mushrooms

1 ounce fresh peas

2 ounces Serrano ham (or prosciutto)

½ cup heavy cream

½ teaspoon curry powder (Madras)

Juice of 1 lemon

4 ounces pea tendrils, for garnish

To make the gnocchi: Place the egg yolks and cheese in the bowl of a stand mixer and blend. While mixing, add the nutmeg, farina and semolina flours, bread crumbs, and salt and pepper. Continue to mix until the dough starts to come together. Remove dough from mixer.

Place all-purpose flour on the kitchen counter or table and work the flour into the dough. Cut off pieces of the dough and roll into long narrow cylinders. Cut the dough into 1-inch pieces.

The gnocchi should be cooked right away in boiling salted water. Cook the gnocchi until they float to the surface. Remove them from water, and place them in a sauté pan over medium-high heat with 2 tablespoons olive oil and the butter. Cook until just golden brown.

In a large sauté pan over medium heat, heat remaining 1 tablespoon olive oil. Add the chanterelles and cook for 2 or 3 minutes. Add the peas and ham. Toss to warm the ham throughout. Add the cooked gnocchi and season with salt and pepper. Combine the cream and curry powder in a small saucepan, and reduce by a quarter. Add the lemon juice, season with salt and pepper, and blend with an immersion blender, incorporating air in the sauce by moving the blender up and down.

Place a tablespoon of sauce each in small pasta bowls and arrange the gnocchi and vegetables on the sauce. Garnish with the pea tendrils and serve immediately.

Opal Restaurant & Bar

1325 State Street, Santa Barbara
(805) 966-9676
www.opalrestaurantandbar.com
Owners: Tina Takaya and Richard Yates

Here's sage advice: When searching for a new restaurant in town, ask the locals. After all, if the locals keep coming back, it must be good. In Santa Barbara, one such place is Opal Restaurant & Bar. Here, you will find California- and Asian-inspired cuisine using the freshest wholesome ingredients. Even the menu suggests "Local Favorites," like the warm seafood salad and lemongrass-crusted salmon. Also recommended are wood-fired pizzas like the Spicy Filet Mignon Pizza, which are delicious and perfectly blistered around the edges, thanks to the blast-furnace heat generated by the Italian pizza oven.

"As soon as you set foot inside Opal, you'll know you are in for a special experience," says Tina Takaya, proprietor of the stylish eatery, which she co-owns with business partner Richard Yates. "Our customers want more than good food, so we try and go that extra mile for them."

The same holds true with Opal's intimate bar—which can get quite crowded and loud on weekends—where you can dine from the regular menu or simply enjoy a glass of fine wine from neighboring Santa Barbara wineries. Some prefer a more innovative cocktail whipped up by the expert Opal mixologists, such as a Thai-chee-ni (Thai chile-infused vodka balanced with lychee fruit), a Fresh Ginger Mandarin Cosmo, a Blood-Orange Greyhound, or a Washington Apple (Crown Royal with apple liqueur, cranberry, and a kiss of lime). The choice is yours.

Black Pepper–Crusted Seared Ahi Tuna with an Amazuke Cucumber Salad on Crispy Wontons with Wasabi Cream

SERVES 6

Amazuke salad:

1/3 cup pickled ginger (pink is best for presentation)

2 cucumbers, peeled, seeded, and cut into 1/8-inch-thick slices (remove alternating strips of peel for presentation)

1 red bell pepper, julienned

1/4 red onion, shaved as thin as possible

1/2 cup rice wine vinegar

1/8 cup sesame oil

Wasabi cream:

2 tablespoons wasabi powder

3 tablespoons water

2 tablespoons sour cream

Tuna:

1 1/2 pounds sushi-grade ahi tuna

Freshly ground black pepper, as needed

Extra-virgin olive oil, as needed

Wontons:

18 wonton skins, cut into rounds
Canola or vegetable oil, for frying

Fresh radish sprouts, for garnish
Toasted black sesame seeds, for garnish

To make the salad: Combine the ginger, cucumber, bell pepper, onion, vinegar, and sesame oil in a bowl. Toss well to combine and set aside.

To make the wasabi cream: Combine the wasabi powder, water, and sour cream. Mix well and set aside. (It will be easiest to use if you pour it into a squeeze bottle.)

Cut the tuna into 2 x 3-inch pieces. Dredge the pieces in black pepper. Prepare a very hot pan with a little extra-virgin olive oil. Sear the ahi on all sides, keeping the fish as rare as possible. Remove from heat and put the tuna in the refrigerator. Slice into ¼-inch-thick slices just before plating.

In a very hot shallow pan with ¼-inch deep of canola or vegetable oil, flash (quick) fry all the wonton skins. Make sure the skins do not roll up; they should stay very flat (use a bacon press or the bottom of another frying pan to help with this). Remove from heat and drain on paper towels. Set aside.

Plating can be done ahead of time if you add the crispy wontons just before serving. On 6 plates, place 3 wontons each in a triangle shape. Place a handful of the salad in the middle. Arrange 3 or 4 slices of tuna around the salad. Draw a circle with the wasabi cream around the tuna and salad. Top with the radish sprouts and sprinkle with toasted black sesame seeds.

WHICH WINE WITH FISH?

Red wine with meat and white with fish. Simple, right? Well, maybe not so much. Old rules have been tossed out like a used wine cork, leaving pairing possibilities wide open. The key to choosing which wine to serve with fish is the preparation and flavor intensity of the food—in general, match a delicate, simple dish with a subtle wine and a more intensely flavored dish with a more powerful wine.

Serving grilled halibut or other white fish? You might try a Sauvignon Blanc, Chenin Blanc, or Pinot Grigio. These versatile white wines are also good with fattier fish, like striped bass, and even shellfish. Sauvignon Blanc also marries well with a creamy New England clam chowder. If you prefer a fuller wine, try sipping a Chardonnay, Viognier, Fumé Blanc, or Pinot Gris.

Wines with a hint of sweetness, like Riesling or Gewürztraminer, stand up well to Asian or spicy dishes. Light reds such as Pinot Noir or Grenache go nicely with heavier sauces and with salmon, tuna, swordfish, and bluefish. Rosés also work with heavier sauces and tomato-based soups; if you prefer a white with your cioppino, try Chablis or Riesling. If all else fails, pop the cork on a good bubbly—sparkling wines like Champagne, Prosecco, and Cava are a match made in heaven with fried seafood and many other fish dishes. Cheers!

Warm Pesto Sautéed Bay Scallop Salad

This is the locals' favorite—toasted pine nuts and fresh grated Parmigiano-Reggiano on a baby spinach salad with roasted garlic dressing.

SERVES 6

Garlic dressing (this recipe will make more than needed):

¼ cup fresh garlic cloves, brushed with a little olive oil and roasted in oven until lightly brown
2 medium eggs
1 tablespoon Dijon mustard
½ cup red wine vinegar
¼ teaspoon cayenne pepper
½ teaspoon salt
2 cups corn oil

Homemade pesto (this recipe will make more than needed):

4 fresh garlic cloves
2 ounces fresh sweet basil, chopped
½ cup extra-virgin olive oil

Salad:

1 pound fresh baby spinach
1/8 cup extra-virgin olive oil
1½ pounds fresh bay scallops
3 ounces whole pine nuts, toasted
Salt, to taste
6 ounces Parmigiano-Reggiano, freshly grated

To make the garlic dressing: Combine the garlic, eggs, mustard, vinegar, cayenne pepper, salt, and corn oil in a blender. Blend until smooth and combined. Place in a container with a lid and refrigerate until needed.

To make the homemade pesto: Combine the garlic and basil in a food processor. Slowly add the olive oil while blending, and blend until combined.

In a large mixing bowl, toss the baby spinach with 5 ounces of the garlic dressing. Divide among 6 plates and set aside.

Using a large sauté pan, heat the extra-virgin olive oil until very hot. Add the bay scallops and sear each side for 45 seconds. Add 5 tablespoons pesto, the toasted pine nuts, and salt to taste. Spoon equal amounts of scallops over the plated spinach salads. Sprinkle a generous ounce of Parmigiano-Reggiano on each and serve.

STONEHOUSE AT SAN YSIDRO RANCH

900 SAN YSIDRO LANE, SANTA BARBARA
(805) 565-1700
WWW.SANYSIDRORANCH.COM
OWNER: TY WARNER

Looking for a true "Santa Barbara experience" like no other? Visit the San Ysidro Ranch.

Hidden within the Montecito foothills is one of the most historic and famous getaways for the rich and famous. It's also home to one of the most amazing culinary experiences, which is why serious foodies flock to the Stonehouse, located within the meticulous grounds of the luxurious property.

Led by executive chef Jamie West, who prefers to grow many of the herbs and vegetables in his own garden, the Stonehouse delivers consistently good food that is well presented. Accompanied by the Ranch's breathtaking vistas, a cozy fireplace, and high-vaulted ceilings, a reservation here cannot go wrong. If you prefer Friday or Saturday evenings, be sure to make a reservation early; if you happen to get lucky, know the restaurant will be very crowded. Otherwise, evenings during the week are equally enjoyable (if not better, thanks to a little extra elbow room).

But all this fuss does not mean the menu is full of fussy food. In fact, the menu is quite unpretentious. With items such as the "famous" tortilla soup, spaghetti, and grilled cheeseburgers, there's definitely a homey feel to this place. For the more discriminating palate, try the butter-braised Maine lobster, the Moroccan-spiced lamb rack, or the classic steak "Diane."

Enjoy your meal outside on the upper deck so you can dine while watching the sun dip over the horizon. As they say, some experiences in life are priceless, and dining at the Stonehouse within San Ysidro Ranch is definitely one of them.

CREAMY BLUE CHEESE POLENTA WITH ROSEMARY & GRILLED PORTOBELLO MUSHROOM

SERVES 4–6

Creamy polenta:

3 tablespoons olive oil

½ cup diced onion

4 garlic cloves, chopped

2 teaspoons chopped fresh rosemary

4 cups water or vegetable stock

1 cup quick-cooking polenta (cornmeal)

½ cup blue cheese (such as Point Reyes)

½ cup half-and-half

Salt and freshly ground black pepper, to taste

Grilled portobello mushroom:

1 tablespoon chopped fresh garlic

½ cup olive oil

¼ cup balsamic vinegar

1 teaspoon chopped fresh rosemary

Salt and freshly ground black pepper, to taste

4 large portobello mushrooms, stems removed, cleaned, and gills scraped

Garnish:

¼ cup diced tomatoes

Extra-virgin olive oil

Blue cheese (such as Point Reyes)

4–6 rosemary sprigs

To make the polenta: Heat a 4-quart saucepan over medium heat. Add the olive oil, onion, and garlic. Sauté for about 3 minutes. Add the rosemary and vegetable stock. Bring to a boil and add the polenta slowly while whisking. Once everything is incorporated, reduce the heat and continue to stir with a wooden spoon. Cook until the polenta is the consistency of thick oatmeal, approximately 5–8 minutes. Remove from heat and stir in the blue cheese and the half-and-half. Taste for seasoning, and add salt and pepper as needed. Keep warm until ready to serve.

In a bowl, combine the garlic, olive oil, vinegar, rosemary, and salt and pepper. Mix well to combine. Add the mushrooms, toss to coat, and let marinate for 15–20 minutes. Cook mushrooms in a grill pan or on a charcoal or gas grill over medium heat until the mushrooms are softened, approximately 4–5 minutes per side. Set aside. The mushrooms can be sliced if desired.

To serve: Place a spoonful of the soft polenta in the center of a small serving plate. Place a mushroom on top of the polenta. Garnish with diced tomato, a drizzle of extra-virgin olive oil, blue cheese, and a sprig of rosemary. Serve immediately.

Tortilla Soup

SERVES 8–10

4 cups plus 3 tablespoons corn oil, divided

4 corn tortillas, each cut into 8 triangles

3 corn tortillas, cut into strips, for garnish

1 medium onion, chopped

4 garlic cloves, chopped

2 dried ancho peppers, seeded and rinsed

1 teaspoon ground cumin

4 ripe tomatoes, chopped

16 ounces tomato juice

1 bay leaf

3 tablespoons chopped fresh oregano

8 cups chicken broth

Salt, to taste

Cayenne pepper, to taste

1 avocado, diced, for garnish

1 cup shredded cheddar cheese, for garnish

1 tablespoon chopped fresh cilantro, for garnish

6 ounces chicken breast, grilled and diced, for garnish

1 lime, cut into 8 wedges, for garnish

Heat the 4 cups of corn oil in a 2-quart pan over medium-high heat for approximately 5 minutes. Add the cut tortilla triangles in batches, and cook until golden brown and crispy. Drain on a paper towel. Cook the thin strips of tortilla in the corn oil and remove when light brown and beginning to crisp. Place on a paper towel.

Heat the remaining 3 tablespoons of corn oil in a 4-quart pan over medium heat. Add the onion and garlic, and cook for 5 minutes, stirring occasionally. Add the crisp tortilla triangles, ancho pepper, and cumin, and continue cooking 5 additional minutes. Add the tomatoes and tomato juice and bring to a boil (this may splatter, so be careful), then add the bay leaf, oregano, and chicken broth. Season with salt and cayenne pepper and let simmer for 20 minutes, stirring to make sure nothing sticks to the bottom of the pan. Blend in a blender (in small batches to prevent soup from overflowing), then adjust the seasoning if necessary. The soup can be made a day ahead and kept refrigerated; reheat when ready to serve.

Pour soup into soup bowls and garnish with the avocado, cheese, cilantro, and chicken. Place some of the crisp tortilla strips on top and squeeze in lime just before eating.

HEARTY PASTA

Pasta is synonymous with Italy, so what better way to honor this celebrated food than to showcase a selection of delectable recipes from some of Santa Barbara County's popular eateries, including three notable Italian trattorias—Palazzio, Piatti, and Trattoria Grappolo?

Most chefs admit that today's store-bought pastas are excellent substitutes for home cooks who don't have the time to hand-make their own pasta. They work well with seasoned sauces (which should not be store-bought; processed versions are loaded with salt and sugar). Also remember that you should never smother your noodles with sauce—add just enough to marry the tender noodles with the wonderful flavors of the homemade topping.

This chapter's pasta dishes are made from the heart and are light and flavorful. The recipes' beauty lies in their simplicity, especially after a long day at the office.

The Enterprise Fish Company, one of Santa Barbara's most recognized seafood restaurants, invites you to try two signature seafood-infused pastas: a shrimp and scallop fettuccine and a Sicilian-style seafood pasta made with fresh shrimp, mussels, and squid. The Los Olivos Cafe and Wine Merchant, just north of Santa Barbara, offers a savory risotto—Roasted Blueberry Risotto with Malvarosa—a dish that definitely represents California goodness. Palazzio, a famous Italian eatery that continues to rack up the awards, emphasizes authentic family-style cooking with Papa Ruby's Pasta and a unique spin on the classic macaroni and cheese. Piatti Ristorante & Bar also focuses on traditional Italian favorites, such as Beef & Pepper Ragu and Chicken Meatballs with Marinara Sauce. Down in Carpinteria (a quaint oceanside city just south of Santa Barbara), Sly's combines abundant California market squid with a zesty marinara in its popular Spaghettini with Calamari in a Spicy Red Sauce. And Trattoria Grappolo, the celebrity-studded Italian bistro in Santa Ynez, where Leonardo Curti has created his own line of pasta sauces, wine, and cookbooks, features three favorite pasta dishes: Naked Ravioli, Rolled Eggplant with Capellini, and Tortelloni with Pumpkin—a tender pumpkin ravioli made with wonton skins!

ENTERPRISE FISH COMPANY

225 STATE STREET, SANTA BARBARA
(805) 962-3313
WWW.ENTERPRISEFISHCO.COM
OWNERS: MICHAEL BANK AND RANDY LAFERR

Near the end of State Street, beside the train station, looms a monumental brick building with a tall smokestack. Once a laundry plant of yesteryear, today it's the well-liked Enterprise Fish Company, clearly recognizable by the large sign and pink, yellow, and blue painted fish out front.

Inside is a charter captain and fish lover's paradise. Painted murals brim with sea life, fish nets and buoys sway from the rafters, and saltwater aquariums bubble and amaze. Taxidermied marlins and salmon—as well as a great white shark head and a full-size deep-sea diver—attract the interested eye. Enterprise Fish Company is where you come to dine on the freshest of seafood amidst one of the most authentic and marine-inspired settings in Santa Barbara.

"We were two childhood friends out of college with big plans," say owners Michael Bank and Randy LaFerr. "We found a nostalgic location in Santa Barbara and built an exhibition kitchen so we could cook our fish slow over a hot mesquite grill, just like we experienced in Mexico."

Michael and Randy's commitment to seafood and service remains unchanged, and they always care about the quality of the fish and seafood they serve. The fresh catches noted on a large blackboard change daily. Come in for the popular happy hour, and for lunch, too. There's generally more seating available then (dinners get busy and often require a wait) and daily specials and discounted fare reward early arrivals. Parking can be a bit tricky, so plan ahead.

SHRIMP & SCALLOP FETTUCCINE

This classic recipe has been a staple at the restaurant for a decade and has caused many a "seafood and cheese" naysayer to see the light. A simple combination of garlic, Parmesan, and cream creates a rich velvety sauce, perfect for a quick, fulfilling meal.

SERVES 4–6

1 pound fettuccine
¼ cup olive oil
5 garlic cloves, minced
½ pound shrimp tails, peeled and deveined
½ pound bay scallops
¼ teaspoon kosher salt
¼ teaspoon white pepper
½ cup white wine
1 cup heavy cream
1½ cups freshly grated Parmesan
2 fresh plum tomatoes, seeded and diced
1 bunch fresh Italian parsley, finely chopped

Cook the pasta in a large pot of boiling salted water until al dente.

While the pasta is cooking, heat a large sauté pan over medium-high heat. Add the olive oil and garlic, and sauté until the garlic is tender and fragrant. Avoiding spatters, gently add the shrimp, scallops, salt, and pepper to the pan. Sauté, but do not allow shrimp to cook through.

Deglaze the pan with wine and then let reduce almost completely. Add the cream and bring to a boil. (It's best not to leave the stove at this stage, as the cream will boil over very easily.) When cream is boiling, immediately add the cooked fettuccine and 1 cup of the Parmesan. Toss to evenly coat, and cook until the sauce thickens. As it cooks, the combination of the pasta absorbing some of the liquid and the cheese thickening it will create a silky smooth sauce. Remove from heat.

To serve: Portion the pasta using tongs, twirling it onto the plate to create height. Then, using a large serving spoon, portion the shrimp, scallops, and sauce over the pasta. Garnish with the remaining Parmesan, diced tomato, and chopped parsley. Serve immediately.

Sicilian-Style Seafood Pasta

It's hard to beat fresh, seasonal seafood with a hearty spicy tomato sauce and pasta ... it's absolutely perfect any time of day. Enterprise Fish Company prepares the sauce for this popular dish every week in giant batches using a giant stainless steel gas-fired kettle.

The sauce holds very well for a week in the refrigerator and for three months in the freezer. For the seafood, feel free to substitute for the options listed here with other favorites. Include a crusty sourdough to soak up the sauce and pair with a sweet and spicy red wine.

SERVES 4–6

Sicilian sauce (makes about 3 quarts—more
than needed, but the sauce freezes well for
use later):

2 cups yellow onions, quartered
2 cups red bell pepper, stemmed and seeded
4 (28-ounce) cans whole tomatoes in juice (such as
    San Marzano)
4 garlic cloves, roughly chopped
1 tablespoon dried basil
1 tablespoon dried oregano
1 tablespoon crushed red pepper flakes
1 teaspoon salt

Seafood pasta:

1 pound penne
¼ cup olive oil
2 garlic cloves, minced
½ cup white wine
1 pound shrimp tails, peeled and deveined
1 pound mussels, cleaned and beards removed
1 pound squid, cleaned and cut into ¼-inch rings
¼ teaspoon kosher salt
Pinch of white pepper
5 cups Sicilian sauce (recipe below)
1 cup freshly grated Parmesan
Lemon wedges, for garnish
1 bunch fresh Italian parsley, finely chopped

To make the sauce: Finely chop (but do not puree) the onions and red peppers in a food processor. Heat a large pot over medium heat, and then add the olive oil and onion and red pepper mixture and sweat until onions are translucent. While the onion and peppers are cooking, submerge a clean hand in the tomato cans to squeeze and break up the whole tomatoes (this is very therapeutic). Add the garlic to the pot and cook until tender. Then add the tomatoes, herbs, red pepper flakes, and salt. Bring to a boil, and then let sauce simmer for 2 hours, stirring occasionally.

Cook the pasta in boiling salted water until al dente.

While the pasta is cooking, bring a large, wide, shallow pot to medium-high heat. Add the olive oil, and then the garlic, and sauté until garlic is tender and slightly charred. Deglaze the pot with the wine and reduce by half. Add the seafood, salt, and pepper, and then cover and cook until the mussels begin to open. Add the Sicilian sauce, stir to incorporate, and bring to a boil. When sauce is boiling, immediately add the

pasta and half of the Parmesan. Toss to evenly coat and continue cooking until mussels have fully opened. The dish should be of a stew-like consistency (not dry).

Using a large slotted spoon, portion as desired and arrange the seafood decoratively over the pasta (discard any unopened mussels), and then spoon remaining sauce over the dish. Garnish with the remaining Parmesan, a lemon wedge, and chopped parsley. Serve immediately.

GOING GREEN IN SANTA BARBARA

Santa Barbara is a "green machine." Nature dapples the city with earthy hues of green. Farmers' markets are filled with locally grown greens. As for the residents, well, many of them have plenty of "green." But Santa Barbara is also heralded as the birthplace of the "green" movement.

In 1969 a major oil spill off the coast of Santa Barbara caused several grassroots organizations, including Get Oil Out (GOO), to join to protect the environment from future spills. The late senator Gaylord Nelson visited Santa Barbara during the spill and was so dismayed by the damage that he quickly conceived and promoted the idea of Earth Day as an educational solution.

Santa Barbarans glommed onto the idea by creating a citywide celebration of Earth Day (www.SBEarthDay.org) every April. In the early 1990s, a slew of Santa Barbara agencies gathered together to create the Green Award Consortium. This consortium works to recognize and promote local businesses that are focusing on protecting the environment (www.greendifference .org). It also seeks to teach citizens how to lessen our impact on the environment through water conservation, organic pest control, and green building construction, to name a few.

Santa Barbara aims to be environmentally conscious right to its core. After all, with a panorama as breathtaking and pristine as Santa Barbara's, it makes sense that insiders are constantly trying to protect it.

Los Olivos Cafe and Wine Merchant

2879 Grand Avenue, Los Olivos
(888) WINES4U (888-946-3748)
www.losoliveoscafe.com
Owners: Sam and Shawnda Marmorstein

If you ever visit laid-back Los Olivos (forty minutes north of Santa Barbara), make a note to duck into the Los Olivos Cafe and Wine Merchant for a savory lunch or dinner or to buy a bottle of wine from their impressive collection of local labels.

Featured in the Academy Award–winning movie *Sideways*—as are a handful of other restaurants in the area—Los Olivos Cafe and Wine Merchant offers exceptional California cuisine with down-home hospitality. After all, you are in the country. Take a seat next to the glass-encased fireplace or at the oversize bar where service is just as swift. On sunny days—and it's virtually always sunny in Los Olivos—request a table outside (these tables are the most sought-after, so it's best to call ahead for a reservation). On the patio, feast on artisan pizzas, hearty pastas, lamb shanks, and short ribs while people watching or simply enjoying your leisurely day in wine country. All of the food at the cafe is local, organic, and sustainable, so it's nice to know that owners Sam and Shawnda Marmorstein care about the environment and what's being passed on to you.

The Marmorsteins also operate a several-acre vineyard and winery, Bernat, which is perfectly situated behind their home. "It's a patient process making wine," the Marmorsteins admit. "All of our grapes are hand-harvested and barrel-aged until they're ready to be born." Next time you're in Los Olivos, make a point to try their certified organic wines along with one of their countrified meals.

Roasted Blueberry Risotto with Malvarosa

SERVES 4

6 cups vegetable stock

3 tablespoons butter

1 medium white onion, finely chopped

2 cups risotto rice (carnaroli or arborio)

¾ cup white wine

2 cups blueberries

2 sprigs fresh thyme

Salt and freshly cracked black pepper, to taste

1 teaspoon mascarpone

Juice of 1 lemon

1 tablespoon fines herbes mixture (tarragon, parsley, chives, and chervil)

Extra-virgin olive oil, for garnish

Freshly grated Malvarosa or Manchego (sheep's-milk cheese), for garnish

In a pot over medium-high heat, bring the vegetable stock to a boil. Preheat the oven to 400°F.

Meanwhile, melt the butter in a sauté pan over low heat. Add the onion and cook for 5 minutes, or until softened. Add the rice and cook, stirring constantly, until the grains are coated in butter. Sprinkle in the wine and cook until the wine has evaporated.

Next, put the blueberries in an ovenproof pan, along with the thyme and a little salt. Place in the oven and roast until the berries blister slightly.

Add a ladleful of the hot stock to the rice and cook, stirring, until the liquid has been absorbed. Continue adding the stock, one ladleful at a time, and stir until each addition has been absorbed. This will take about 18–20 minutes. Once all the stock as been absorbed, season to taste with salt and fresh cracked pepper.

When the rice is tender, stir in the mascarpone, lemon juice, and fines herbes, and transfer to a warm serving dish.

Garnish with the roasted blueberries and a drizzle of extra-virgin olive oil, and serve with fresh grated Malvarosa or Manchego.

Palazzio

1026 State Street, Santa Barbara
(805) 564-1985
www.palazzio.com
Owner: Kenneth Boxer

Palazzio, a bustling Italian eatery where a beehive of activity abounds, lies along the famous Santa Barbara strip—known as State Street. Whether you're seated at the bar or one of the cloth-covered tables in this establishment, the energy is contagious and the food is authentic.

"At Palazzio our guests are treated as if they were a part of our family," says owner Kenneth Boxer. "Our food and drink portions are enormous—probably the largest you'll find in Santa Barbara. As a result, nobody ever leaves Palazzio hungry or thirsty!" Palazzio is also the only restaurant in the United States that features an authentic full-scale rendition of the Sistine Chapel ceiling, as if Michelangelo himself painted it.

"When our guests arrive at Palazzio, they can feel an energy and excitement like they would attending an opening night Broadway performance," adds Boxer. "They will have an incredibly memorable dining experience that will remain with them for a lifetime. This is what excites me the most."

With its large, diverse menu, Palazzio offers diners some of the best Italian food the city has to offer at very reasonable prices. If there's still room for dessert, be sure to order the Ronald Reagan Presidential Tiramisu. Palazzio served this very dessert to the president at his Los Angeles presidential office.

PAPA RUBY'S PASTA

SERVES 4

Grilled chicken:

2 large boneless, skinless chicken breasts
1 teaspoon chopped fresh rosemary
1 tablespoon Worcestershire sauce
3 teaspoons olive oil

Roasted bell peppers sauce (makes about 2 cups roasted peppers):

7 red bell peppers
3 tablespoons olive oil, for greasing baking sheet
1 teaspoon salt
1 teaspoon white pepper
5 cups heavy cream

Pasta:

1 pound spaghetti
2 ounces sun-dried tomatoes
4 ounces artichoke hearts

Preheat the oven to 350°F.

Dice the chicken breasts. Place in a bowl and add the rosemary, Worcestershire, and olive oil. Toss well to combine. Transfer to refrigerator and allow to marinate for at least 3 hours.

Split the peppers in half, and arrange them on an oiled sheet pan. Bake the peppers for about 20 minutes until soft and blistered. Let cool for 10 minutes. When cool, remove the skins and place the red peppers in a blender. Season with salt and white pepper and add the cream. Set aside.

Place the chicken on a hot outdoor barbecue or grill. You can also use a large nonstick pan over high heat. Grill or cook until chicken is tender and cooked through. Remove from heat.

Cook the pasta in boiling salted water until al dente. Drain and then transfer the pasta to a large sauté pan over medium heat. Add the sun-dried tomatoes and diced chicken, and then add the artichoke hearts and roasted bell pepper–cream mixture. Toss well to combine, and cook for 3 or 4 minutes, until everything is incorporated and hot. Remove pasta from heat, transfer to individual bowls, and serve immediately.

Macaroni & Cheese

SERVES 6

½ large yellow onion, peeled and diced
2 tablespoons olive oil
1 pound macaroni
2 cups cream
3 cups freshly grated Parmesan
3 cups smoked mozzarella cheese
1 cup Gorgonzola
5 eggs, beaten
3 ounces prosciutto, finely diced

In a sauté pan over medium heat, add the olive oil and diced onion. Sauté until the onions have broken down and carmalized. Set aside.

Preheat the oven to 350°F.

In a pot of boiling salted water, cook the macaroni until al dente (about 8 minutes on high heat). Remove from heat and drain.

Transfer the macaroni to a large bowl. Add the caramelized onions, cream, Parmesan, mozzarella, Gorgonzola, eggs, and prosciutto. Stir for about 2 minutes, until well mixed.

Transfer the macaroni and cheese to a casserole dish and place in the oven. Bake for about 35 minutes, or until golden brown on top.

Remove macaroni and cheese from the oven and cut into six pieces. Serve immediately.

BOCCE: SANTA BARBARA'S WINE-FRIENDLY SPORT

Let the good times roll! The game of bocce and wine go together like spaghetti and meatballs. The objective of the game is to get your (or your team's) balls as close to a fixed target as possible, but an equally important goal is to soak up the high spirits and good fellowship that surround the game.

Many wineries have added bocce courts and encourage visitors to play while they sip. Wineries in the Paso Robles area sporting bocce courts include Donati Family Vineyard, Eberle Winery, Robert Hall Winery, and Silver Horse. At Coquelicot Vineyard in Los Olivos you can taste a top-notch Sangiovese or Sauvignon Blanc on the tree-shaded patio while watching or playing a game.

The early Romans were among the first to play bocce, and the modern-day game was developed in Italy, so it seems only fitting that an Italian restaurant is the go-to spot for bocce action. Arnoldi's Café, one of the oldest restaurants in Santa Barbara, boasts two courts where you can play bocce between your bruschetta and your bolognese, all without having to put down your glass of Barolo.

Piatti Ristorante & Bar

www.piatti.com

Owner: Moana Restaurant Group

In the hills of ritzy Montecito, Piatti Ristorante & Bar invites you to experience a slice of Tuscany. From the bright and cheerful mustard walls to the rustic tiles on the expansive floor to the elegant white tablecloths, this place screams Italy. The open kitchen and stone pizza hearth invite guests to gather around to savor a seasonally driven menu complemented by an extensive list of Central Coast wines.

Piatti offers three unique and equally inviting dining areas. The main dining room features a fireplace that adds warmth and ambiance, especially on a cool, drizzly evening. The patio offers year-round outdoor dining beside a slow-flowing creek under gigantic eucalyptus trees. And off the dining room is Piatti's al fresco "island," covered by canvas umbrellas (during the day) and lit by the stars and candles at night.

Executive chef Edward Huante is a firm believer in serving nothing but the best when it comes to fresh, local ingredients, which begins with supporting sustainable fishing and farming practices. And the patrons dining at Piatti can almost taste the chef's culinary passion as they dine on some of his favorite dishes, like the classic osso bucco, short ribs, oxtail, and ragus along with slow-cooked, braised dishes that entice with the most seductive of aromas.

Recently, the Piatti Montecito location closed its doors, making way for Montecito Wine Bistro Pierre LaFond (which also has a location on State Street in downtown Santa Barbara). Because Chef Huante is an extraordinarily talented individual and an exalted steward of the environment, we had to share his famous meat ragu and meatball recipes. These two delicious dishes were Piatti favorites—and now hopefully will become favorites in your home.

Beef & Pepper Ragu

SERVES 4–6

Salt and freshly ground black pepper, as needed
All-purpose flour, as needed
2 tablespoons olive oil
2½ pounds beef top round, cubed
1 medium yellow onion, finely diced
4 garlic cloves, thinly sliced
1 pasilla chile, seeded and diced
1 red bell pepper, seeded and diced
1 fennel bulb, cored and diced
2 cups white wine (preferably Chianti)
2½ pounds canned peeled tomatoes with basil
1 sprig fresh rosemary, stemmed and minced
2 bay leaves
2 cups beef or chicken stock

Pasta or gnocchi

Preheat the oven to 350°F. Salt and pepper and lightly flour the beef cubes.

On the stove top, heat the olive oil in a large ovenproof pot over medium-high heat. Brown the beef cubes until they are slightly crispy on the outside. Remove the beef from the pot and add the onion. Reduce heat to medium and sauté the onion until tender and translucent. Add the garlic and cook until lightly brown. Add the peppers and fennel, and cook until tender. Add the white wine and bring up to a simmer. Add the tomatoes, rosemary, bay leaves, and stock and bring up to a simmer. Add the beef cubes.

Once the sauce is simmering again, cover with an ovenproof lid and transfer to the oven for 1 hour. Remove the pot from the oven, and with a whisk, beat the sauce to break up the meat and tomatoes. Return to oven for 1 more hour, and then repeat the process of breaking up large chunks. Season with salt and pepper to taste.

Serve the ragu with pasta such as penne or orecchiette. This sauce also goes well with gnocchi.

CHICKEN MEATBALLS WITH MARINARA SAUCE

SERVES 4–6

Marinara sauce:

1½ cups diced yellow onion

1 tablespoon olive oil plus ½ cup to finish sauce

¼ cup sliced garlic

8 pounds ripe tomatoes (preferably heirloom), peeled

15 fresh basil leaves

½ bunch fresh Italian parsley, stemmed

Salt and freshly ground black pepper, to taste

Chicken meatballs:

1 tablespoon butter

½ tablespoon olive oil

½ cup diced yellow onion

1 tablespoon diced fresh sage

8 ounces ground prosciutto

2 cups stale bread (¼-inch dice)

¼ cup heavy cream

2 eggs

2 egg yolks

2 pounds ground chicken

2 tablespoons chopped fresh Italian parsley

Salt and freshly ground black pepper, to taste

Olive oil, for frying

All-purpose flour, as needed

To make the marinara sauce: Sauté the onions in 1 tablespoon olive oil in a thick-bottomed pot until tender and translucent. Add the garlic and cook until lightly brown. Add the tomatoes, basil, and parsley, and bring sauce up to a simmer. Simmer sauce until the tomatoes break down and the sauce begins to thicken, at least 2 hours. Finish by whisking in salt, pepper, and about ½ cup olive oil.

To make the chicken meatballs: Combine the butter, olive oil, onion, sage, and prosciutto in a sauté pan over low heat. Sauté slowly until onions are soft and translucent and the prosciutto is crispy. Remove from heat and refrigerate.

In a mixing bowl, combine the bread crumbs, cream, eggs, and egg yolks. Refrigerate for at least 30 minutes to chill.

In a large mixing bowl, combine the onion mixture with the bread crumb mixture. Add the ground chicken and parsley, and season with salt and pepper. Mix all the ingredients together for about 3 minutes, until well combined.

Roll the meatballs into 2-ounce portions. Fill a large sauté pan halfway with olive oil. Heat over a very low flame. Lightly flour the meatballs and, using tongs, carefully place the meatballs in the hot oil. The heat should be low enough that the meatballs take about 10 minutes to brown and cook through. Remove finished meatballs from heat, and drain on paper towels. Set aside and keep warm.

Serve the meatballs with the marinara sauce and your favorite noodle. Spaghetti and linguini are the traditional choices.

SLY'S

686 LINDEN AVENUE, CARPINTERIA
(805) 684-6666
WWW.SLYSONLINE.COM
OWNERS: JAMES AND ANNIE SLY

Within the compact beach community of Carpinteria (ten minutes south of Santa Barbara) lies a golden brick building emblazoned with the words SEAFOOD, STEAKS AND COCKTAILS above the arched entryway. Welcome to Sly's, a newly remodeled establishment that's ready to serve you.

Celebrating their third year in business, Sly's owners James (formerly a chef at Lucky's) and Annie Sly continue to offer their big menu to the masses, including the famous "Blue Plate Specials." Meat Loaf Monday and Short Ribs Saturday are definitely the most sought-after, according to the throngs of beach lovers (and local celebs like Kevin Costner) who pack the place full on those days. Then again, thanks to the restaurant being within walking distance of many homes and condos, Sly's is at capacity virtually any day. It's no surprise that word of James's good-quality comfort food and hospitable service quickly got around the neighborhood.

Open seven days a week, Sly's will serve breakfast and brunch for those wanting to begin the morning right. And in California you can never go wrong with a plate of huevos rancheros or "Dutch Baby" pancakes.

Full-service dining is also available in the popular wood-clad bar, where Sly's is also well known for its vintage cocktails. After all, there are only a handful of restaurants in Santa Barbara where you can order a Harvey Wallbanger or a real Tom Collins and find a bartender behind the counter who knows how to make one.

Spaghettini with Calamari in a Spicy Red Sauce

This is a fast, simple, and delicious pasta to make—and a popular one at Sly's. If you have the marinara sauce already made (or if you cheat and buy a jar), the entire process can take as little as twenty-five minutes, most of which is waiting for the water to boil. Naturally, you can make the dish as spicy or as mild as you like—and if, like one of the regular customers at Sly's, you prefer linguini to spaghettini, well, the process is exactly the same.

SERVES 4

Marinara (yields about 3 cups):

½ cup yellow onion, finely chopped

2 tablespoons extra-virgin olive oil

1 teaspoon chopped fresh garlic

1 bay leaf

Salt and freshly ground black pepper, to taste

⅛ tablespoon crushed red pepper flakes

⅛ tablespoon dried oregano

⅜ cup dry red wine

1 can (28-ounce) peeled and crushed tomatoes (San Marzano)

3 fresh basil leaves, coarsely chopped

Pasta:

1 pound small calamari (with tentacles), cleaned

Salt and freshly ground black pepper, to taste

2 teaspoons crushed red pepper flakes

1 pound spaghettini (thin spaghetti)

¼ cup olive oil

2 tablespoons coarsely chopped fresh Italian parsley

In a thick-bottomed nonreactive pan (e.g., stainless steel) over medium heat, sweat the onions in the olive oil until they are soft and golden. Add the garlic, and sweat for 1 minute over low heat. Add the bay leaf, salt and pepper, red pepper flakes, and dried oregano. Pour in the red wine. Add the tomatoes and bring to a simmer. Cook, stirring occasionally, for

25 minutes. Remove from heat, and stir in the basil. Adjust the salt and pepper if necessary. Keep sauce warm.

Slice the calamari into ¼-inch rings. Sprinkle with salt, pepper, and red pepper flakes (with the amount depending on your heat preference).

Bring a large pot of water to a boil. Salt heavily (i.e. about 5½ tablespoons). Cook the pasta until al dente, then drain, reserving a little of the pasta water, about ¼ to ⅜ cup.

Return the drained spaghettini to the warm pot with the reserved pasta water. Heat the olive oil in a large, shallow, thick-bottomed sauté pan over high heat. When hot, carefully add the calamari while stirring. The oil will pop, so be careful. Cook calamari for no longer than 30 seconds. Carefully add the warm marinara sauce, and then add the pasta and pasta water. Toss well to combine.

To serve: Arrange the pasta on warm plates, and top with the Italian parsley.

CALIFORNIA MARKET SQUID

Launched in Monterey Bay in the 1860s, the market squid fishery is one of the oldest in California. Chinese fishermen rowed skiffs at night, blazing torches mounted in the bows to attract the unsuspecting cephalopods; accompanying skiffs netted the squid, which were dried and exported, mainly to China.

Today, squid has become the state's most valuable fishery, with most of the world's harvest coming from California. The market squid is most abundant between Punta Eugenia, Baja, California and Monterey Bay, although they range as far north as Alaska.

Most often called by its more appealing Italian name of calamari, the market squid's meat is firm and white with a mild, slightly sweet flavor. Although the tentacles are edible, the body is the source of the prized meat, which can be stuffed, cut into flat pieces, or sliced crosswise into rings. The picture of versatility, squid is available fresh, canned, frozen, dried, and pickled, and it is suited to a slew of cooking methods. Try it tossed into a hearty paella or robust risotto, fried in cornmeal batter, sautéed with garlic and olive oil, or quickly boiled and chilled in a refreshing salad.

TRATTORIA GRAPPOLO

3687 SAGUNTO STREET, SANTA YNEZ
(805) 688-6899
WWW.TRATTORIAGRAPPOLO.COM
OWNERS: LEONARDO CURTI AND DANIELE SERRA

Ready for authentic Italian food served by a real Italian family surrounded by winemakers, music moguls, and movie stars? You don't have to travel to Los Angeles to find such a place. Head forty minutes north of Santa Barbara to the bucolic town of Santa Ynez to dine at Trattoria Grappolo. Just make sure you have a reservation before you arrive.

Executive chef Leonardo Curti and business partner Daniele Serra are the masterminds behind Trattoria Grappolo—one of the most popular restaurants in Santa Barbara County. Both Curti and Serra were born in Italy and relocated to California, and the two Italians connected when a failing restaurant in the valley needed a makeover. Tired of salvaging failing restaurants, both Curti and Serra agreed it was time to take over and open a restaurant of their dreams. Enlisting the help of Leonardo's younger brothers, Alfonso and Georgio, both chefs, the team opened Trattoria Grappolo in 1997 and has never looked back.

"The key for a successful restaurant is to keep it interesting," says Leonardo, who works the open kitchen with his elite team of cooks. "This makes people come back." But, extravagant as the menu is, some of the most interesting items aren't listed at all. Ordering a special meal "off the menu" is just one of the Trattoria's secrets for devoted guests.

For a more intimate or private celebration, make a reservation for the VIP dining room, which is completely separate from the restaurant. It even comes with its own servers, restroom, and wine cellar.

The two recipes featured in this chapter, along with many more, can be found in Chef Curti's award-winning cookbook: *Trattoria Grappolo: Simple Recipes for Traditional Italian Cuisine.* "And don't worry if you don't have time to hand-make your own pasta," says Curti. "Today's store-bought pastas are excellent substitutes that work very well."

NAKED RAVIOLI

SERVES 4

1 cup cooked, drained, and chopped
    fresh spinach
1 cup ricotta cheese
½ cup grated fresh Parmesan cheese,
    plus more for garnish
1 pinch ground nutmeg
1 clove garlic, minced

1 egg
Salt and pepper, to taste
Italian bread crumbs (as needed)
1 cup flour
Melted butter, for garnish
Fresh sage leaves, for garnish

In a large bowl, combine the spinach, ricotta, Parmesan, nutmeg, garlic, egg, and salt and pepper. If the mixture is too wet, add a handful of bread crumbs, a little at a time. Mix well.

Using a 1-ounce ice cream scoop, scoop the filling into balls. Roll each ball into the flour and coat well.

Bring a large stockpot filled with salted water to a boil. When boiling, add the ravioli balls and cook for several minutes until they float.

Remove the ravioli and serve with melted butter, sage, grated Parmesan, and your favorite sauce.

Rolled Eggplant with Capellini

SERVES 4 (3 ROLLS PER PERSON)

Homemade tomato sauce (makes about 1½ quarts; freeze the extra for use later):

¼ cup olive oil

¾ cup sliced white onion

2 garlic cloves, diced

2 (28-ounce) cans Italian peeled tomatoes (San Marzano)

3 fresh basil leaves

Salt and freshly ground black pepper, to taste

Filling:

1 cup ricotta cheese

1 cup homemade tomato sauce (see recipe above)

4 fresh basil leaves, finely chopped

Pinch of salt

Pinch of freshly ground black pepper

Pinch of dried oregano

1 pound capellini (angel hair pasta)

Eggplant:

2 large elongated eggplant

2 cups all-purpose flour

2 cups olive oil, for frying

1 cup homemade tomato sauce (see recipe above)

12 slices smoked mozzarella cheese

To make the tomato sauce: Combine the olive oil, onion, and garlic in a heavy saucepan over medium-high heat. Cook until the onion turns light golden yellow, about 3 minutes. Add the tomatoes and bring to a boil. Lower heat and simmer for 20–25 minutes. Add the basil leaves, and break the large chunks of tomato with a fork or a whisk. Add the salt and pepper to taste, and set sauce aside.

To make the filling: Combine the ricotta cheese, tomato sauce, basil, salt, pepper, and oregano in a large bowl. Stir to combine. Meanwhile, in a large stockpot of boiling salted water, cook the capellini pasta until al dente. Remove from heat and drain. Add the capellini to the cheese filling and mix well.

Preheat the oven to 375°F.

Thinly slice the eggplant lengthwise, about ⅛ inch thick. Dust each slice in flour and fry in a shallow frying pan with oil until golden brown on each side. Remove finished slices from oil and drain on paper towels.

Line up the slices of eggplant, and place about 1 tablespoon filling in the center of each slice. Roll each eggplant slice and place in a baking dish. Pour the tomato sauce over the rolls. Top each roll with a slice of smoked mozzarella. Bake for about 10 minutes, or until cheese is golden brown. Remove from oven and serve.

SANTA BARBARA'S QUINTESSENTIAL VIEW

A thousand places in Santa Barbara County could vie for the title of "the quintessential view," the one vista that sums up why Santa Barbara is so wonderful.

Yes, there's atop the Riviera for that bird's-eye view of the harbor, a grove of oak trees lit like a cathedral in Santa Ynez, a wildlife beach on Santa Cruz Island with pounding surf and birds orbiting towers of rock. Yet there is one place so extraordinary, so scenic, and so representative that it perhaps deserves to be first among equals. The Hurricane Deck Trail, nestled within the San Rafael Wilderness in the Los Padres National Forest, is a beacon for intrepid campers, hikers, and horseback riders, a mecca for brave urbanites seeking solitude and oneness with nature.

Wildly beautiful and accessible by foot, the Hurricane Deck Trail, with its dense chaparral, canyons, and undulating mountain peaks, is as much a part of the Santa Barbara County experience as are the dazzling shorelines, restaurants, and historical monuments.

Just don't expect a leisurely stroll.

The 217,000-acre San Rafael Wilderness is located in the wild and remote San Rafael and Sierra Madre mountain ranges in Santa Barbara County, just northeast of Los Olivos. This surging terrain ranges from high, snow-covered peaks to dense forest to desert yucca. There are more than 125 miles of roads and hiking trails throughout the vast, protected wilderness, but a few—like the Hurricane Deck Trail, sandwiched between the White Ledge Campground and the Manzana Schoolhouse—deliver the rawest and most primitive views you'll ever discover in central California. Once home to the foraging Chumash people, the Hurricane Deck is traveled by just a handful of seasoned mountaineers each year. Their sole purpose: witnessing extraordinary vistas that could only be seen otherwise from an airplane or helicopter.

Tortelloni with Pumpkin

SERVES 4

1 cup canned pumpkin

1 cup ricotta

¼ cup freshly grated Parmesan

1 tablespoon diced Italian mostarda
(fruit condiment), optional

Dash of ground nutmeg

Salt and freshly ground black pepper, to taste

Italian bread crumbs, as needed

1 package large wonton skins

2 eggs

2 tablespoons butter

5 fresh sage leaves

3 cups heavy cream

4 amaretto cookies, crushed, for garnish

In a large bowl, combine the canned pumpkin, ricotta, Parmesan, mostarda, nutmeg, and salt and pepper. Mix well to combine. If the pumpkin mixture is very wet, add bread crumbs until a drier mixture is achieved. Set aside.

Place the wonton skins on a flat work surface. Using a 1-ounce ice-cream scoop, place 1 scoop of pumpkin mixture in the center of each wonton skin. In a separate bowl, beat the eggs for an egg wash. Dip a pastry brush into the egg wash and brush each interior side of the skin around the pumpkin mixture. Fold into a triangle. Gently press around the filling area to remove any air pockets. Brush the two bottom corners of the triangle with the egg wash, and pull the corners together, one corner on top of the other. Repeat the process until all tortelloni are folded.

In a large saucepan, combine the butter and sage leaves over medium heat. After the butter has melted, add the cream and salt and pepper, and reduce the sauce by one-third.

Meanwhile, in a large stockpot of boiling salted water, cook the tortelloni for about 2½ minutes. Remove tortelloni from heat, drain, and add to the butter and sage sauce. Serve immediately with amaretto cookies on top.

FISH & SHELLFISH

Santa Barbara's proximity to the Pacific Ocean allows the picturesque city to offer a wide assortment of fresh fish and shellfish. According to the California Seafood Council, California fishermen and seafood suppliers deliver about 300 species to market every year.

In the 1980s, the California fishing industry was dominated by the Pacific sardine, and later by the tuna fishery. In the 1990s, California market squid, crab, groundfish, pink shrimp, salmon, sea urchin, spiny lobster, and swordfish kept the industry flourishing. Today, a mixture of species contribute to the volume and value of the California catch.

Some of California's native seafoods include the albacore, California halibut, Dungeness crab, California market squid, Pacific swordfish, pink shrimp, red sea urchin, spiny lobster, and the California spot prawn. And that's good news to Santa Barbara restaurants that enjoy featuring a bevy of seafood on their menus.

In this chapter, Arch Rock Fish, Santa Barbara's "neighborhood joint," shares a signature lobster roll and house-made cioppino. Harbor hangout Brophy Brothers includes a cioppino recipe, too, along with oysters Rockefeller. Kai Sushi, located on downtown State Street, whips up a delicious mango salmon, a fresh sea bass dish, and fried shrimp. Tom and Adam White are proud to showcase recipes from their popular restaurants—FisHouse and Santa Barbara Shellfish Company: a wonton- and sesame-crusted mahimahi and wine-steamed black mussels. Tre Lune, Montecito's premier Italian restaurant, puts a unique spin on things with baccalà alla vicentina, featuring Italian dried cod. And the Wine Cask, nestled in the historic El Paseo complex, makes a splash with its seared diver scallops and incredibly moist Dungeness crab and corn cakes.

ARCH ROCK FISH

608 ANACAPA STREET, SANTA BARBARA
(805) 845-2800
WWW.ARCHROCKFISH.COM
OWNERS: HJL GROUP RESTAURANT ADVISORS

Arch Rock Fish, named after the famous rock on nearby Anacapa Island, is a casual "neighborhood joint" that garners rave reviews from locals and visitors alike.

It doesn't matter whether you arrive for lunch, happy hour, or dinner, because Arch Rock Fish will take care of you while serving some of the freshest seafood around. Beer-steamed mussels, spicy tuna, steamed lobster, and miso cod are just a sampling of some of the delicious items you'll discover. Arch Rock Fish also serves wonderful sandwiches, like the famous lobster roll (featured here) and the house-made cioppino (also featured).

"Any restaurant can feed you or put a drink in front of you, but how many actually care about you?" asks co-owner Jeremiah Higgins. "At Arch Rock Fish, you will find yourself having fun because not only do we serve great food, we've created a friendly gathering place where we will know your name, know what you like to eat, and have an emotional connection with you. That's because we have a real passion for what we do."

The exciting eatery was founded by the HJL Group Restaurant Advisors, led by veteran restaurateur Jeremiah Higgins, celebrity chef Scott Leibfried, and Galaxy-soccer-player-turned-coach Cobi Jones. Mike Anderson is also a partner and serves as beverage director.

All in all, this is a fun place to hang out while enjoying good-quality seafood.

FISH CIOPPINO

SERVES 4

Cioppino base:

1 (28-ounce) can San Marzano whole plum tomatoes

1 tablespoon tomato paste

1 teaspoon onion powder

½ teaspoon dried oregano

½ teaspoon dried basil

1 pinch crushed red pepper flakes (optional)

1 teaspoon granulated sugar

¼ cup chopped fresh basil

½ cup extra-virgin olive oil

Salt and freshly ground black pepper, to taste

Fish and herbs:

1 tablespoon olive oil

2 ounces garlic cloves, sliced (about 6 to 8 cloves)

1 shallot, thinly sliced

2 dozen live black mussels

1 cup white wine

Salt and freshly ground black pepper, to taste

1 cup lobster stock (available at most fish markets or grocery stores)

8 medium to large shrimp tails, peeled and cleaned

½ pound fresh fish trimmings (available at your local fish market)

2 raw lobster tails, split in half (if using cooked lobster, add it later in cooking process)

1 tablespoon chopped fresh parsley

½ cup sliced fresh basil leaves

2 tablespoons extra-virgin olive oil

To make the cioppino base: Combine the tomatoes, tomato paste, onion powder, oregano, dried basil, red pepper flakes (if desired), sugar, fresh basil, and olive oil in a large mixing bowl. Puree with an immersion blender until smooth. If an immersion blender is unavailable, blend in small batches in a blender and combine the batches at the end. Season with salt and pepper and set aside.

Heat a large pot or pan to assemble the entire dish. The same pot or pan can be used to serve the cioppino. Heat a small amount of olive oil over medium heat and sauté the garlic and shallots until tender, about 2 minutes (careful not to burn the garlic). Add the mussels and white wine and reduce by half. Season with salt and pepper. Add the lobster stock, shrimp, fish trimmings, lobster tails, parsley, and cioppino base. Cover and simmer for 3–6 minutes to cook the seafood through. Taste and add salt and pepper if needed. Remove soup from stove, sprinkle the fresh basil over the top, and drizzle with extra-virgin olive oil. Serve immediately.

LOBSTER ROLL

MAKES 4 SANDWICHES

Lobster:

2 lemons, halved

1 cup white wine

2 bay leaves

10 white peppercorns

Salt, to taste

4 live lobsters (1¼ pound each)

Lobster mayonnaise:

1 tablespoon crème fraîche

¼ teaspoon lobster base or paste
   (available in Asian or specialty markets)

½ cup mayonnaise

Zest and juice of 1 lemon

Salt and white pepper, to taste

Butter, at room temperature, as needed

4 soft burger buns (similar to brioche), sliced in half

¼ cup chopped fresh chives

2 cups shredded iceberg lettuce

In a large pot (large enough to fit 4 lobsters), combine the lemons, white wine, bay leaves, peppercorns, and pinch of salt. Prepare a separate large mixing bowl (or fill your sink) with cold water and ice cubes for an ice bath to shock the lobsters, stopping the cooking process. Fill the pot three-quarters full with cold water. Bring to a boil and add the lobsters. Cook the lobsters for 12 minutes, and then carefully remove from the water and add them to the ice bath. Cool for 10 minutes, and then drain the water. Remove the lobster meat from the shells and chop into bite-size pieces. Place the shucked lobster meat in a mixing bowl and refrigerate.

To make the lobster mayonnaise: Combine the crème fraîche, lobster base, mayonnaise, and lemon zest and juice. Mix well to combine, and season with salt and white pepper.

Combine the lobster meat with the lobster mayonnaise. Taste and season with additional salt and white pepper if needed. Refrigerate.

Spread a small amount of butter on both sides of the buns and toast, butter side down, in a nonstick pan until browned and crispy. Place about 4 ounces of the lobster salad on each bun. Sprinkle with chopped chives, add the shredded lettuce, and finish with the top of the bun.

CALIFORNIA SPINY LOBSTER

While it may not have the loveliest name, the California spiny lobster is a shining star in any local seafood popularity contest. Also known as rock lobster, the spiny lobster (which gets its name from the sharp spines across the head and back) is found in shallow, rocky areas from Monterey Bay in the north to Mexico's Gulf of Tehuantepec in the south.

The California spiny lobster has no large front claws, but its firm, sweet meat is similar to that of its distant cold-water cousin. Most of the meat is in its tail, and lends itself well to classic recipes such as lobster risotto, lobster bisque, lobster salad, lobster Thermidor, and lobster Newburg. Tails are also sublime simply brushed with butter and grilled, or steamed or roasted. And it's a cinch to make lobster stock from the body and legs.

"Spinies" are gathered in traps or by hand by divers and sold live in tanks, and they are an excellent sustainable seafood choice. They're available October through March at Santa Barbara area farmers' markets and local fish markets. You may also find vacuum-packed frozen tails in your local market (see photo pn page 12).

Brophy Brothers Restaurant & Clam Bar

119 Harbor Way, Santa Barbara
(805) 966-4418
www.brophybros.com
Owners: John Bennett, James Manar for the Bennett family

Just like the golden beaches, the historic Steams Wharf, and the boat-filled harbor, Brophy Brothers Restaurant & Clam Bar is truly an iconic fixture on the Santa Barbara waterfront. A popular destination for Santa Barbara residents and tourists alike, it's a must-experience eatery for those who haven't yet had an opportunity to visit or enjoy the restaurant's mouth-watering offerings.

So what is it about Brophy's that is so appealing? Fans of the restaurant would argue it's a combination of great food, a lively atmosphere, and an excellent location. Brophy's popular wraparound upper deck offers unobstructed, panoramic views of the ocean and harbor, with the mountains looming in the background. And the Clam Bar is always packed with patrons sipping cold beers, spicy Bloody Marys, and glasses of chilled Chardonnay. The eatery is especially popular as a Friday and Saturday night destination, and has limited dining space and tables, but patience and persistence will pay off, and is certainly worth it. It's best to arrive early and stay late so you can enjoy signature and sustainable Brophy dishes like the local swordfish, oysters on the half shell, peel-and-eat shrimp, the grilled thresher shark sandwich, or a hearty bowl of the celebrated clam chowder.

CIOPPINO

MAKES ABOUT 2 GALLONS (PERFECT FOR LEFTOVERS)

Cioppino base:

1 stick (8 tablespoons) butter
2 leeks, diced
2 pounds yellow onions, peeled and sliced
¼ cup fresh garlic cloves, chopped
4 green bell peppers, seeded and chopped
4 cups diced tomatoes
4 cups tomato sauce
1 teaspoon crushed red pepper flakes
4 bay leaves
2 tablespoons dried thyme
2 teaspoons dried basil
2 teaspoons dried oregano
Salt and freshly ground black pepper, to taste
4 cups clam juice
2 cups white wine

Seafood:

2 pounds fresh red snapper fillets, cut into pieces
2 pounds fresh shrimp
1 pound live mussels
12 live littleneck clams
Parmesan, for garnish
Saltine crackers, for garnish

To make the cioppino base: Melt the butter in a large pot over medium heat. Add the leeks, onions, garlic, and bell peppers, and cook until vegetables are soft and lightly brown. Add the tomatoes and tomato sauce. Add the red pepper flakes, bay leaves, thyme, basil, oregano, and salt and pepper to taste. Stir in the clam juice, reduce heat to a simmer, and simmer for 30 minutes. After 30 minutes, add the wine and cook for 5 additional minutes.

To finish the cioppino: Add the fish, shrimp, mussels, and clams. Increase the heat to high and cook the seafood for 5 minutes, or until the fish is cooked through and the mussels and clams have opened (discard any unopened mussels or clams).

Divide the fish and shellfish among individual serving bowls. Ladle the cioppino base over the seafood. Top with Parmesan and serve hot with saltine crackers.

Oysters Rockefeller

SERVES 6–8

Mornay sauce (makes about 4 cups; this may be more than you need, but all depends on how many oysters you are serving and how large the oysters are):

4 cups milk
¼ cup roux or all-purpose flour (to thicken)
½ pound freshly grated Parmesan
½ teaspoon nutmeg
1 pinch each salt and white pepper
½ cup white wine

Rockefeller mix:

½ pound bacon
4 tablespoons unsalted butter
2 garlic cloves, peeled and minced
¼ pound yellow onion, diced
1¼ pounds fresh spinach, chopped
2 tablespoons white wine
Salt and white pepper, to taste
2 tablespoons Pernod

12–16 fresh oysters
Jack cheese, grated, as needed

To make the Mornay sauce: Add the milk to a saucepan over medium heat. Add the roux or flour, and bring to a boil, stirring continuously. Add the Parmesan and cook until smooth. Add the nutmeg, salt and pepper, and wine. Cook for 10 minutes and then strain the sauce and set aside.

To make the Rockefeller mix: Cook the bacon in a sauté pan over medium heat until lightly brown. Remove the bacon and drain on paper towels. Finely dice.

In the same pan (discard excess grease), melt the butter. Add the garlic and onion, and cook until soft and translucent. Add the spinach, wine, and salt and pepper. Remove from heat and stir in 1¼ cups of Mornay sauce. Allow the mixture to cool. When cool, add the Pernod and bacon.

Open the oysters at the last moment before serving. Serve on a platter chilled in the freezer with crushed ice (or on a bed of frozen rock salt). Top the freshly shucked oysters with 2 tablespoons of Rockefeller mix, 1 teaspoon of Mornay sauce, and some Jack cheese.

HOW TO SHUCK AN OYSTER

Expert shuckers at oyster bars open piles of oysters at lightning speed, making the process look fairly easy. Well, it isn't exactly easy, but with practice (darn, you'll have to eat a few oysters along the way) you can become proficient. Here's how: First, make sure oyster shells are tightly closed to be certain they are still alive. Scrub fresh oysters under cold running water. Hold the oyster firmly on a board, flat side up and covered by a dishtowel. It's best to wear heavy gloves to protect your hands. Place the tip of a good oyster knife into the hinge and dig slowly and firmly with a back-and-forth motion and steady pressure, but not too much force. Remember to keep your oyster-holding hand out of harm's (or the knife's) way. When you feel the knife penetrate the shell, give a twist (you'll hear a little pop as it opens) and slide the knife along beneath the top shell, cutting the muscle. Take off the top shell and slide the knife beneath the oyster to cut the bottom muscle. Always keep the oyster level to hold onto the briny-sweet juices—serve on a bed of crushed ice to keep oysters level and cold. A spritz of fresh lemon, and you're in oyster heaven.

KAI SUSHI

738 STATE STREET, SANTA BARBARA
(805) 560-8777
WWW.KAISUSHISHABUSHABU.COM
OWNER: KAZ SATO

Kai Sushi is located on the bustling corner of De La Guerra and State Street in downtown Santa Barbara, and it is considered one of the city's premier sushi restaurants.

Owner and executive chef Kaz Sato (coauthor of *The Complete Idiot's Guide to Sushi & Sashimi*) is a respected sushi chef. Born in Tokyo, Sato earned his culinary credentials at Shinjuku Culinary School before working at notable establishments in Jogashima—one of Japan's premier fishing areas and fish markets. Sato elevated his career by becoming a chef at the prestigious Tokyo Kaikan, and when he was asked to open a restaurant in Los Angeles (where the California roll originated), the young chef relocated to the United States. After a stint as head chef for Sushi Zen in Portland,

Oregon, Sato returned to California and opened Kai Sushi, named for his son, in 1981. Thirty years later, Sato continues to serve up traditional Japanese cuisine infused with unique artistic flare. From his popular Dragon Roll, bursting with a cornucopia of flavor, to his crunchy Spider Roll and wildly inventive Uni Shooter, Sato is a true artiste. When it comes to entertaining guests with phenomenal cuisine, he is the master.

"Creating delicious Japanese cuisine at home is not as difficult as you may think," says Chef Sato, whom you'll often find behind the counter preparing your sushi. "The ingredients, for the most part, are simple and straightforward, and you can make substitutions based on your individual preferences and tastes."

MANGO SALMON

SERVES 2

Mango sauce:

1 ripe mango, peeled and diced

1½ teaspoons rice vinegar

2 tablespoons cooking sake or light rum

1 tablespoon sugar

1 tablespoon mayonnaise

Pinch of salt

1 teaspoon soy sauce

Salmon:

2 tablespoons sliced Maui onion, sweet onion,
    or red onion

3 thin slices fresh wild-caught Pacific salmon
    (each approximately 2 x 3 inches)

12 strands daikon radish sprouts (kaiware),
    cut in half

Smelt eggs or flying fish roe, for garnish

Sesame seeds, for garnish

To make the mango sauce: Put the mango in a blender and blend until smooth. Add the vinegar, sake or rum, sugar, mayonnaise, salt, and soy sauce. Blend until incorporated.

Divide the onion slices into 3 equal parts. Top each salmon slice with onion. Roll each salmon slice, onions on the inside, carefully with your fingers, and cut the salmon roll in half with a sharp, moistened knife.

Arrange the six sliced salmon rolls on a plate and top with the radish sprouts. Place a dollop of the mango sauce on top of each roll, and garnish with a sprinkle of smelt eggs or flying fish roe and sesame seeds.

Japanese Sea Bass with Garlic Soy Sauce

SERVES 2

Garlic soy sauce:

2 tablespoons sesame oil

1 garlic clove, sliced

2 tablespoons soy sauce

2 tablespoons cooking sake

2 tablespoons water

Pinch of green onion

1–2 dashes chili powder

Sea bass:

1–2 large shiitake mushrooms, sliced

1 piece fresh sea bass, approximately 1 x 4 inches,
    ½ inch thick

1 garlic clove, thinly sliced

1 asparagus spear, sliced into long pieces on the
    diagonal

1 small handful of enoki mushrooms

1 block of tofu, approximately 2 x 4 inches,
    1 inch thick

Sesame seeds, for garnish

To make the garlic soy sauce: Heat the oil in a saucepan over medium heat and cook the garlic until softened and golden. Add the soy sauce, sake, and water. Stir well. Add the green onions and chili powder. Stir again, and let cook for several minutes. Remove from heat and reserve.

On a baking sheet lined with foil, arrange the shiitake mushrooms and place the sea bass alongside. Top the bass with garlic. Place the asparagus beside the bass. Drizzle the mushrooms, bass, and asparagus liberally with the garlic soy sauce. Place the baking sheet in a toaster oven or under the broiler for 4–5 minutes, or until bass is half-cooked. Add the enoki mushrooms to the baking sheet. Cook until the fish is opaque and tender, about another 5 minutes, and remove from heat.

Meanwhile, heat the tofu by either microwaving it or submerging it in a pot of boiling water. When it is thoroughly heated, place the tofu block in the center of a large serving plate. Place the bass and garlic atop the tofu. Spoon the shiitake mushrooms over the bass. Lean the asparagus and enoki mushrooms against the tofu and sea bass. Drizzle with remaining cooking juices, and finish with a sprinkle of sesame seeds.

EBI FRIED SHRIMP

In Japanese, fried shrimp is called ebi-fry. Scallops make an excellent alternative. Buy large sea scallops, and slice them in half lengthwise to speed up the deep-frying process.

SERVES 2

4 large cold water shrimp, cleaned,
    shelled, and deveined
3 cups vegetable oil

Creamy sesame dressing:

2 tablespoons ground sesame seeds
1 teaspoon rice vinegar
1 teaspoon vegetable oil
1 teaspoon sugar
1 teaspoon soy sauce
1–2 teaspoons mayonnaise

1 cup flour, for dusting
2 eggs, beaten
1 cup plain bread crumbs (or panko)
2 cups green cabbage, chopped

With a sharp knife, butterfly the shrimp by slicing them nearly in half, being careful not to completely sever the halves. Heat the oil over high heat in a deep fryer, pot, or pan.

To make the creamy sesame dressing: Mix the sesame seeds, vinegar, oil, sugar, soy sauce, and mayonnaise in a bowl and chill until ready to serve.

Dip each shrimp in flour and shake off the excess. Next, dip each in egg, then bread crumbs, coating well.

Carefully place each battered shrimp into the hot oil and deep-fry until crisp and golden brown.

Mound the cabbage in the center of a serving plate and arrange the fried shrimp on top. Drizzle with the creamy sesame dressing and serve.

Santa Barbara FisHouse

101 East Cabrillo Boulevard, Santa Barbara
(805) 966-2112
www.sbfishhouse.com
Owners: Tom and Adam White

Santa Barbara is synonymous with fresh fish, and many of the most desirable seafood eateries in town can be found near or along the waterfront. One in particular, the Santa Barbara FisHouse, is located directly across from Stearns Wharf.

Part casual, part elegant, the FisHouse attracts a variety of patrons—those coming in off the beach and those planning a special night out. Despite the typical seafood restaurant decor—stuffed game fish, rods and reels, nautical tables, aquariums—the food does impress. You can always expect the freshest of fish and shellfish, much of which is caught in local waters, including spiny lobster, sea bass, halibut, and crab. Because owners Tom and Adam (Tom's son) White care about where their seafood comes from, you'll also find many healthy and sustainable species on the menu, like the salmon, tuna, clams, and mussels.

The FisHouse is a laid-back restaurant with postcard views and friendly service, and it seems you can always find a table. If you prefer not to dine inside with a marlin looming over your head, request a seat outside on the patio. The setting is much more romantic and, as at most of the restaurants in Santa Barbara, there are plenty of heat lamps and even a fire pit to keep you warm if the temperature starts to dip. A few more tips for visiting the FisHouse: There's plenty of parking in the lot in the back if you don't find parking out front, the restaurant is very kid friendly, and, for those who like their happy hours, the often-crowded bar offers great specials like half-price Maine lobster. If you need a recommendation for lunch or dinner, order the macadamia nut–encrusted sea bass and a blood orange margarita.

Wonton- & Sesame-Crusted Mahimahi with Pineapple Fried Rice & Roasted Red Pepper Beurre Blanc

SERVES 2

Pineapple fried rice:

1 tablespoon olive oil

2 tablespoons diced red or sweet onion

¼ cup diced bell peppers (a mixture of red, orange, and yellow)

⅓ cup diced fresh pineapple

1 cup cooked long-grain rice

3–4 tablespoons oyster sauce (teriyaki sauce can be substituted)

Red pepper beurre blanc:

1 red bell pepper

2 cups white wine

1 bay leaf

8–10 black peppercorns

4 sprigs fresh thyme

1 shallot, chopped

¼ cup heavy cream

1⅓ sticks unsalted butter

1 tablespoon fresh lemon juice

Salt and freshly ground pepper, to taste

Fish:

Oil, for frying

4 small wonton wrappers

¼ cup sesame seeds (a mixture black and white is most attractive, but one color is fine)

1 pound fresh boneless, skinless mahimahi fillet

Salt and freshly ground black pepper, to taste

1 tablespoon olive oil, for cooking fish

To make the pineapple fried rice: Heat the olive oil in a sauté pan over medium-high heat. Add the onion, bell peppers, and pineapple. Cook until tender. Add the rice, stirring occasionally. Add the oyster sauce and let cook for 2 minutes. Set aside and keep warm.

To make the red pepper beurre blanc: Begin by roasting the bell pepper. This can be done on the stovetop or under the broiler. Roast all sides until charred and blistered. Remove pepper from heat. When cool, chop the pepper, discarding the seeds.

In a small pot over medium heat, combine the wine, roasted bell pepper, bay leaf, peppercorns, thyme, and shallots. Reduce until almost dry. Add the cream, and continue to reduce. Lower the heat and add the butter slowly, whisking constantly. Add the lemon juice and salt and pepper to taste. Strain through a fine strainer and keep warm.

Preheat the oven to 450°F. Heat frying oil in a skillet and fry the wontons quickly, just until crispy. Remove the wontons with a slotted spoon and drain on paper towel. When cool, crush the wontons into fine crumbs. Transfer the crumbs to a plate. Put the sesame seeds on a second plate. Next, slice the fish fillet into two equal portions. Season the fillets with salt and pepper, and roll in the crushed wontons, and then the sesame seeds, until well coated. Heat the olive oil in an ovenproof pan over medium-high heat, add the fish, and cook for 1 minute on each side. Remove from heat and transfer to the oven. Cook for about 6–8 minutes, or until fish is cooked through.

Arrange the fish on two serving plates and top with the red pepper beurre blanc. Spoon the pineapple fried rice alongside and serve immediately.

Santa Barbara Shellfish Company

230 Stearns Wharf, Santa Barbara
(805) 966-6676
www.sbfishhouse.com
Owners: Tom and Adam White

The most visited landmark in Santa Barbara is Stearns Wharf. It is here where locals and tourists come to stroll, shop, fish, eat, and marvel at some of the city's most spectacular views, from the Riviera and gold sand beaches to the neighboring Channel Islands.

At the end of the famous—but rather touristy—wood-planked pier is a charming little seafood shack known as the Santa Barbara Shellfish Company. If the glass tanks outside stuffed with rambunctious lobster and crab brought in daily by the local fishermen don't entice you, step inside.

Here you can watch the skilled chefs busily at work in the open kitchen, plopping lobsters down on the grill or plucking massive Santa Barbara spider crab out of bubbling cauldrons. While you peruse the daily specials on the chalkboard menu, don't forget to claim your seat. If you can actually find an empty barstool along the counter, you may have to arm-wrestle for it, as this place is typically congested, and the chairs are almost always spoken for. But don't worry—there are better seats outside, particularly at one of the roomy picnic tables in front of the restaurant, where you can dine with the sun cascading down and a brown pelican perched on the railing begging for a scrap.

Many come here for the chowder, which is one of the Shellfish Company's popular items. You can get a cup or have it served in a bread bowl. The steamed clams, mussels,

crab, and lobster are also a hit. But if you ask any of the locals who frequent this place for recommendations, they'll almost always give you the same response: The two items that have people coming back are the shrimp and lobster tacos. You will not find a better tasting seafood taco in Santa Barbara. Just ask owners Tom and Adam White. You can often find them here during lunch hour, feasting on the prized tacos.

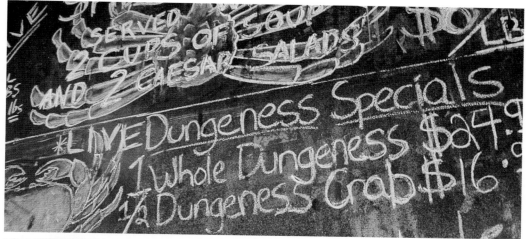

Steamed Black Mussels

SERVES 2

1 pound fresh black mussels

1 tablespoon olive oil

2–6 garlic cloves, chopped

1 shallot, thinly sliced

1 small pinch crushed red pepper flakes

Fresh tarragon, to taste

White wine (Chablis or Chardonnay; enough
　to cover the mussels)

Juice of ½ lemon

Butter, to taste

Sourdough bread (optional)

Wash the mussels under cold running water, and peel away the beards attached to the shell if they haven't already been removed.

Heat the olive oil in a large sauté pan over medium-high heat. Add the garlic and shallot, and sauté until the garlic and shallot are soft and golden. Add the red pepper flakes, tarragon, and mussels. Add the white wine and lemon juice, and cook until mussels begin to open. Add as much butter as you like, and continue cooking until the mussels are completely open. Discard any unopened mussels.

Transfer the mussels and broth into two large serving bowls. If desired, serve with crusty sourdough bread that's been grilled with butter and garlic.

FARMED MUSSELS: A BETTER ALTERNATIVE

Europeans have been happily slurping up mussels for ages, but Americans have been a bit slower to embrace this briny-sweet bivalve. Until recent years, farms in Canada and New Zealand have been major sources for mussels in the United States. But American aquaculturists, buoyed by the increase in popularity and demand, have begun farming the delicacies in the Northeast and along the Pacific coast, from California to Alaska.

Aquaculture represents an eco-friendly and sustainable alternative to wild mussels. Mussels are mainly grown on ropes hanging from rafts, so the ocean floor isn't disturbed. Farms produce cleaner mussels, without seabed grit, and controlled waters mean fewer diseases; chemicals and antibiotics are rarely used in mussel farming. Another plus: mussels filter the water as they feed, so they leave the water cleaner than they found it.

Versatility is the mussel's middle name. Quickly simmered with white wine and garlic, they are simple and delicious, but they can also be smoked, steamed, boiled, roasted, barbecued, or fried in butter. Choose mussels that are tightly closed or that close when tapped, and discard any with cracked shells.

TRE LUNE

1151 COAST VILLAGE ROAD, MONTECITO
(805) 969-2646
OWNER: GENE MONTESANO

Montecito is well known for its stylish, upscale eateries, and one that continues to impress is the Italian trattoria Tre Lune (meaning "three moons").

Easy to spot on Coast Village Road—look for the sugar-white walls with blue-trimmed windows and a terra cotta tiled roof—Tre Lune is a neighborhood restaurant that seems to cater to Montecito regulars. It's not really the optimum choice for starving students, although a visit will make you feel like a million bucks. From the house-made bread and olive oil to the brightly flavored minestrone soup and the fall-off-the-fork osso bucco, Tre Lune delivers authentic and traditional Italian to its affluent clientele. Wild boar penne, basil pesto, and lobster ravioli are standouts, as is the all-Italian wine list, a yearly *Wine Spectator* award winner. Frittatas, breads, and other breakfast treats also add an appealing extra dimension in the morning. If you intend to dine here, be sure to make a reservation or arrive early; the place does get crowded and sometimes a bit loud. Also take a moment to admire the vintage photographs of Hollywood glitterati on the walls, like the one at right of Dean Martin and John Wayne.

The dish featured here—baccalà alla vicentina—is from Vicenza, Italy, and made with dried cod. In most baccalà dishes, the cod needs to be soaked multiple times to remove excess salt used in the drying process. However, baccalà alla vicentina is made from dried unsalted cod, also referred to in the culinary world as stockfish.

BACCALÀ ALLA VICENTINA

SERVES 6

3 pounds dried cod (stockfish)

1 tablespoon olive oil

1 pound white onions, thinly sliced

2 garlic cloves, chopped

2 anchovy fillets (packed in oil), drained and chopped

1 sprig fresh Italian parsley, chopped

All-purpose flour, for dredging

Freshly grated Parmesan, for dredging

1 cup milk

1 cup extra-virgin olive oil

Polenta, for serving

Begin by soaking the cod in fresh water for 2–3 days, changing the water every day. When the cod is finished soaking, remove from the water and pat dry. Cut the cod into 3-inch pieces.

Preheat the oven to 350°F.

In a sauté pan over medium heat, heat the olive oil. Add the onions and garlic, and sauté until soft and tender, about 5 minutes. Add the anchovy and parsley. Reduce heat to low and sauté for an additional 5 minutes. Remove from heat.

In the bottom of a casserole dish, spread half of the cooked onions.

In a mixing bowl, combine equal parts flour and Parmesan. Dredge the cod pieces into the flour-Parmesan mixture and shake off excess. Layer the cod pieces close together on top of the onions in the casserole dish. Spread the remaining onions on top of the cod, forming a third layer. Gently pour the milk and olive oil over the top, being generous with the liquid. Cover the casserole dish with aluminum foil and bake for 2 hours, occasionally shaking the dish gently. Uncover the dish and continue to bake another 30 minutes, or until golden brown.

Remove from oven and let rest. Serve with soft or grilled polenta.

WHAT'S IN A NAME

Ever wondered about the different regions on the labels of Santa Barbara wines? These appellations, also known as American Viticultural Areas (AVAs), can divulge much about the character of the wine you are about to drink. If a label says SANTA YNEZ VALLEY, this means at least 85 percent of the grapes were grown in that federally recognized region. It's a guarantee of geographic origin. Once you know a bit about the growing conditions in these areas, you'll have a richer appreciation for the differences in climate and soils that create the flavor of the wine. California has sixty-nine appellations, four of which are located in Santa Barbara County.

Santa Rita Hills—In 2001 the Bureau of Alcohol, Tobacco, and Firearms approved this AVA to differentiate wines made from grapes grown on the cooler western edge of the Santa Ynez Valley. Conditions here mirror those of Reims in Champagne, France. Morning fog is frequent, winds are strong, and soils typically contain less clay and more calcium than those in the east-

ern Santa Ynez Valley. World-class Pinot Noir and Chardonnay are produced in this region, which encompasses most of the vineyards west of Highway 101.

Santa Ynez Valley—Lying predominantly east of Highway 101, this region is generally warmer than the Santa Rita Hills area, with well-drained soils ranging from sandy loams and clay loams to shaly and silty clay loams. The area primarily produces high-quality Cabernet Sauvignon, Cabernet Franc, Merlot, Syrah, Grenache, and Sauvignon Blanc.

Santa Maria Valley—This funnel-shaped region in the northern part of Santa Barbara County has a cool climate, thanks to its prevailing ocean winds, and enjoys one of the longest growing seasons of any viticultural area in the world. The area's well-drained soils range from sandy loam to clay loam, and its cool temperatures make it one of California's best AVAs for Pinot Noir and Chardonnay. Rhone varietals also thrive here, showing great clarity (crystal clear and without sediment) and depth of fruit (complexity or layers of flavor).

Happy Canyon—The most recently minted AVA in Santa Barbara County, Happy Canyon sits on the eastern edge of the Santa Ynez Valley. Higher temperatures and a mineral-rich growing environment (*terroir*) produce excellent Bordeaux varietals—Cabernet Franc, Cabernet Sauvignon, Merlot, Petit Verdot, and Sauvignon Blanc—as well as Rhone varieties like Syrah.

WINE CASK

813 ANACAPA STREET, SANTA BARBARA
(805) 966-9463
WWW.WINECASK.COM
OWNERS: DOUG MARGERUM AND MITCHELL SJERVEN

If you wander through the beautiful outdoor courtyard of historic El Paseo, you'll stumble upon a well-known restaurant and tasting room frequented by locals—the Wine Cask.

Like many restaurants in Santa Barbara, the Wine Cask supports local farmers and purveyors by buying from those who support the environment through organic and sustainable practices while also delivering the freshest and healthiest products possible. The same can be said for the restaurant's vast wine selection, which comes from many nearby vineyards and wineries. Whether you're dining outside under the white arches or white umbrellas, or inside in the "Gold" room, Intermezzo Bar, or private "Riviera" room, the Wine Cask is a food and wine pairing experience.

"Many guests who dine with us not only prefer good-quality ingredients, but they can really taste the difference," says executive chef Brandon Hughes. A local chef who trained and honed his culinary skills in Santa Barbara, Chef Hughes takes his job at one of area's best-known restaurants very seriously: "That's why I believe in using the freshest ingredients possible while developing creative menus that not only inspire but also represent the culinary tradition of the Wine Cask."

The best seats in the house are the tables next to the fireplace. If you're in the bar, head for one of the sofas by the fire. It's all about ambiance and atmosphere here, so you'll find yourself enjoying your Wagyu New York strip with house-made bacon and wild mushroom hash or the crispy-skin salmon with sautéed spinach surrounded by a warm and inviting vibe. You'll be certain to stop the hostess on the way out to make your next reservation.

Seared Diver Scallops with Fava Beans, Pancetta, Mint & "Cured" Fennel Salad

SERVES 6

18 fresh sea scallops

2 cups shelled fava beans

1 head fennel

Juice of 1 lemon

¼ cup extra-virgin olive oil

1 teaspoon sea salt

½ pound pancetta, cubed

2 tablespoons butter

3 large shallots, cut into thin rings

5 mint leaves

Salt and freshly ground black pepper, to taste

¼ cup white wine

¼ cup canola oil

Set the scallops on paper towels to absorb excess water, and transfer to the refrigerator.

In a pot of heavily salted boiling water, cook the fava beans for 1 minute. Strain the beans and set in an ice water bath to shock the beans (immediately stopping the cooking process). Once cold, remove the beans from the ice water and remove the skin from each bean. Set the beans aside.

Slice the fennel as thin as possible (a Japanese mandolin works best). Place the sliced fennel in a bowl, and add the lemon juice, olive oil, and sea salt. Squeeze the fennel in the liquid for 1 minute. This will help "cure" the fennel. Set aside.

In a large, hot sauté pan over medium heat, cook the pancetta. Sauté until browned, then add the butter, shallots, and fava beans. Cook until the beans are tender. Add the mint and salt and pepper to taste. Add the white wine and deglaze pan. Remove from heat and keep warm.

Heat the canola oil in two large sauté pans over very high heat until they are screaming hot. Season each scallop with sea salt. Place the scallops in the pans, and brown on one side, and then turn them over. The Wine Cask prepares the scallops medium rare, but cook them as you like.

To serve: Arrange three scallops on each plate, and then place the warm fava bean sauté next to the scallops. Arrange the fennel atop the beans and serve immediately.

Dungeness Crab & Corn Cakes with Rustic Tomatillo & Pasilla Salsa & Cilantro Aioli

SERVES 6

Crab cakes:

2 tablespoons butter
1 cup fresh sweet corn kernels
1 small red onion, diced
Salt and freshly ground black pepper,
    to taste
2 pounds fresh Dungeness crabmeat
¼ cup panko bread crumbs
Juice of 1 lime
1 egg
Canola oil, for sautéing

Tomatillo and pasilla salsa:

1 pound fresh tomatillos, peeled and washed
2 pasilla chiles
Juice of 1 lime
Salt and freshly ground black pepper,
    to taste

Cilantro aioli:

1 jalapeño
3 egg yolks
2 large garlic cloves, minced
1 tablespoon kosher salt
1 tablespoon Dijon mustard
1 tablespoon white vinegar
Juice of ½ lemon
½ bunch fresh cilantro, finely chopped
1 tablespoon extra-virgin olive oil
1½ cups canola oil

To make the crab cakes: Melt the butter in a sauté pan over medium heat. Add the corn and red onion, and cook until onion is soft. Season with salt and pepper, and set aside to cool.

Once cooled, place the corn-onion mixture in a large bowl. Add the crabmeat, bread crumbs, lime juice, egg, and additional salt and pepper. Mix well to combine (but don't break up the crabmeat; you want it to stay in lumps). Let the mixture sit for 30 minutes so the bread crumbs soak up moisture and help firm the crab cakes. Form the cakes into 2-inch-wide and 1-inch-tall cakes.

Pan-fry the cakes in canola oil over medium-high heat until the cakes are golden brown on each side. Remove from heat and drain on paper towel. Keep warm.

To make the salsa: Blister or roast the tomatillos and pasillas on a grill or in a very hot sauté pan until tender. Remove from heat and place in a food processor with the lime juice. Pulse until chunky. Add salt and pepper to taste. Set aside.

To make the cilantro aioli: Blister or roast the jalapeño on a grill or in a very hot sauté pan until tender. Remove from heat and let cool. When cooled, split the pepper with a knife and remove the seeds. Dice the pepper. (Using gloves or washing hands immediately after handling the pepper is recommended.)

In a mixing bowl, combine the egg yolks, garlic, salt, mustard, vinegar, lemon juice, roasted jalapeño, cilantro, and olive oil. Stir well to combine. Slowly add the canola oil while whisking.

To serve: Arrange crab cakes on individual serving plates. Smear the cilantro aioli under each cake and top with the tomatillo and pasilla salsa.

MEAT & POULTRY

Fresh, wild, and hearty are perfect adjectives to describe the tender meats and juicy poultry Santa Barbara County chefs prepare night in and night out. Without question, these award-winning restaurants and their culinary teams rule the grill. Chefs Jeff and Matt Nichols of Brothers Restaurant—Sides Hardware and Shoes admit that their love of meat stems from their Iowa roots, which set the foundation for their passion. The brothers are also influenced by the area's storied history of cowboys and land-grant ranches, which is reflected in the menu.

Alisal Guest Ranch & Resort, recognized for perfect meats grilled over Alisal oak, starts it off with Beer-Braised Pot Roast with Root Vegetables, the perfect comfort food for a cold night at home. For those more cheerful days, try the resort's crisp and tender Chinese Chicken Salad. Chef Budi Kazali of the Ballard Inn is inspired by the outdoor wilderness, so he contributes Pan-Seared Duck Breast with Sweet Potato Puree & Cherry Pinot Noir Sauce—a stunning presentation, indeed. He also offers a grilled quail and an Australian rack of lamb. The Brothers Restaurant—Sides Hardware and Shoes keeps to the hearty theme by showcasing Grilled Fillet of Prime Beef with Stilton Cheese & Port Wine Sauce along with Pinot Noir–Braised Short Ribs.

Santa Barbara's Ca'Dario Ristorante emphasizes California cowboy fare, epitomized by the Quail with Sausage & Polenta, Pan-Roasted Chicken Breast, and Roasted Rack of Lamb recipes. Seagrass Restaurant, well known for its full range of beef (as well as sustainable seafood), encourages home cooks to try its lip-smacking Braised Garlicky Short Ribs. Finally, former Trattoria Grappolo chef Alfonso Curti makes his cookbook debut with three heralded recipes from his popular restaurant Trattoria Uliveto—Sliced New York Steak over Arugula with Shaved Parmesan, Osso Bucco alla Milanese, and Sautéed Veal Chop with Morel Mushrooms & Brandy.

ALISAL GUEST RANCH & RESORT

1054 ALISAL ROAD, SOLVANG
(805) 688-6411
WWW.ALISAL.COM
OWNERS: THE JACKSON FAMILY

Santa Barbara may have the San Ysidro Ranch, but Santa Ynez Valley is proud to call the Alisal Guest Ranch & Resort its premiere destination resort.

Since 1946, the Alisal has been catering to visitors seeking the ultimate in accommodations, spas, and fine dining in the heart of wine country. When hunger strikes after a leisurely day of golf, horseback riding, fly fishing, tennis, or wine tasting, make a reservation at the Ranch Room or the River Grill, both located inside the lavish resort. Buttermilk fried chicken, shepherd's pie, and barbecue salmon are just several of the artistic comfort foods you'll find, along with pan-fried Cornish game hens, braised lamb shanks, and beer-braised pot roast with root vegetables (the featured recipe here).

Executive chef Pascal Godé (pronounced go-DAY) enjoys leading a kitchen inspired by the ol' West, coupled with fresh organic ingredients supplied by many local farmers and ranchers. Because the Ranch is surrounded by award-winning wineries, there are plenty of exceptional bottles to pair with Pascal's ranch-style cuisine.

When you find yourself in the valley and are looking for a satisfying home-style meal amid the rolling hills and serpentine oak trees, visit the Alisal Guest Ranch & Resort. You can gather around outdoor barbecues as if you were invited to a friend's backyard. Hearty pancake breakfasts and live music in the River Grill Bar are two additional draws that keep the Alisal Guest Ranch & Resort ranked as one of the top dining venues in the valley.

Beer-Braised Pot Roast with Root Vegetables

SERVES 6

6 chuck eye rolls (12 ounces each)

12 slices bacon

Salt and freshly ground black pepper, to taste

Steak rub or seasoning, to taste

Olive oil, for searing

1 medium yellow onion, sliced

1 cup diced celery

1 cup diced carrot

1 cup diced fresh tomato

5 garlic cloves, smashed

1 bay leaf

2 sprigs fresh thyme

1 quart veal stock

1 quart beer

¼ cup chopped fresh Italian parsley

Roasted root vegetables:

1 medium celery root, peeled and cut into 1-inch cubes

4 carrots, peeled and cut into 1-inch cubes

4 parsnips, peeled and cut into 1-inch cubes

⅓ cup extra-virgin olive oil

Kosher salt and freshly ground black pepper, to taste

Preheat the oven to 300°F.

Wrap each beef portion with 2 slices of bacon and secure with kitchen twine. Season with salt and pepper and the steak rub or seasoning. Add olive oil and wrapped beef to a large ovenproof braising pan over high heat. Sear the meat on all sides, until deep golden brown, and then remove meat from pan and set aside.

In the same pan, sauté the onion, celery, and carrot for about 4 minutes. Add the tomato, garlic, bay leaf, thyme, veal stock, and beer. Reduce the liquid by one-third. Return the seared beef to the pan and transfer to the oven for approximately 1½ hours. Turn the beef over halfway through the cooking process.

On a baking sheet, toss the celery root, carrots, and parsnips with the olive oil and season with salt and pepper. Roast in a preheated 400°F oven, stirring occasionally, until the vegetables are browned and tender, about 25–30 minutes. (Note: This can be done while the beef is cooking if you have a double oven or after the beef is cooked if a single oven.)

Remove the meat from the pan and reduce the braising juices at least by half. Remove and discard the twine and bacon from the meat. On a platter, arrange the meat in the center, with the roasted root vegetables around, and spoon some juices on top of the meat. Sprinkle with parsley. You might want to prepare your favorite mashed potatoes to serve with the pot roast.

CHINESE CHICKEN SALAD

SERVES 6

Sesame-ginger vinaigrette:

3 tablespoons Chinese mustard

½ cup sesame oil

¼ cup olive oil

¼ cup honey

½ cup light soy sauce

1 cup rice wine vinegar

1 medium piece fresh ginger, grated

1 garlic clove, chopped

1 tablespoon hoisin sauce (available in Asian groceries)

½ tablespoon sweet chili paste

Salt and freshly ground black pepper, to taste

Chicken salad:

1 medium Napa cabbage, washed and shredded

1 medium iceberg lettuce, washed and thinly sliced

1 medium romaine lettuce, washed and chopped

1 red bell pepper, julienned

1 green bell pepper, julienned

1 cup snow peas, sliced

3 green onions, chopped

1 cup carrots, peeled and shredded

1 cup bean sprouts

6 chicken breasts (6 ounces each), cooked and diced

Crispy wontons (available in Asian groceries),
    for garnish

¼ cup fresh cilantro, chopped

2 tablespoons white sesame seeds, toasted

To make the sesame-ginger vinaigrette: Put the mustard in a blender, and then add the sesame oil, olive oil, honey, soy sauce, rice wine vinegar, ginger, garlic, hoisin sauce, sweet chili paste, and salt and pepper (go light on salt because of the soy sauce). Give it a quick blend and check the seasoning.

In a bowl, combine the cabbage, lettuces, peppers, snow peas, green onions, carrots, bean sprouts, and diced chicken. Toss together with the sesame-ginger vinaigrette until well combined. Divide the salad among 6 plates and garnish with crispy wontons, cilantro, and sesame seeds.

SOLVANG

The Danish-American village of Solvang has been drawing visitors for decades to its well-kept streets dotted with Scandinavian-themed architecture, windmills, and Danish delights around every geranium-draped corner. The charming European-style town, nestled in the heart of Santa Barbara's wine country, with the Santa Ynez Mountains as a backdrop, boasts courtyards and squares jam-packed with shops, inns, restaurants, open-air cafes, Danish bakeries, chocolate shops, a craft beer brewery, wine tasting rooms, art galleries, and museums paying homage to the town's Danish heritage.

Solvang's Scandinavian roots go back to 1911, when Danish-American settlers arrived in the Santa Ynez Valley seeking a place where their crops, dairy cows, and culture could flourish in the California sun. They founded the town of Solvang ("sunny field" in Danish), and today that agricultural heritage is celebrated with a popular weekly farmers' market and more than a dozen wine tasting rooms.

The circa-1804 Old Mission Santa Inés, a National Historic Landmark, showcases the area's Spanish history—it was the first Spanish settlement in the Santa Ynez Valley and is still an active parish today.

Guided tours of the town are offered via a replica of a circa-1915 streetcar trolley drawn by a pair of Belgian draft horses. Visitors also browse the Hans Christian Andersen Museum or Elverhoj Museum of History & Art, the Solvang Vintage Motorcycle Museum, or the Quicksilver Miniature Horse Ranch, or take a hike at the picture-perfect Nojoqui Falls County Park.

And along with the old-world hospitality, nearly everyone samples the Danish delicacy of *aebleskiver*, light and airy pancake balls dusted with powdered sugar and served with raspberry jam.

THE BALLARD INN

2436 BASELINE AVENUE, BALLARD
(805) 688-7770
WWW.BALLARDINN.COM
OWNERS: THE KAZALI FAMILY

Nestled in the heart of Ballard—a charming little suburb in the Santa Ynez Valley—one of the most elegant and romantic B&Bs in town has staked its claim. Behind the white picket fence and flowery grass courtyard is the quaint, family-style, two-story Ballard Inn. Considered one of the most sought-after small luxury accommodations in central California, the Inn is well known for its award-winning French-Asian cuisine.

With only a dozen candlelight tables arranged beneath the gold light fixtures and a wood-mantled fireplace, this intimate dining room can't begin to serve everyone in town (even outside on the patio overlooking the fragrant rose garden), so reservations are a must.

What makes dining at the Ballard Inn so special—other than the fabulous food—is the personal connection executive chef and owner Budi Kazali has with this charming restaurant. Because of the limited number of guests, Chef Kazali puts his heart and soul into every dish and personally follows up tableside to make sure you are pleased. Virtually every guest who makes a reservation here boasts about the impressive menu, including local foie gras, crispy barramundi flown in fresh from Australia, and grilled beef tenderloin.

One of the most popular entrees on the menu, according to Chef Kazali, is the pan-seared duck breast with sweet potato puree and cherry Pinot Noir sauce (featured here), which has been called the chef's signature dish. "The duck breast is perfectly seared to medium-rare," says Chef Kazali with a smile. "The cherry Pinot Noir reduction pairs beautifully with many of the local Pinot Noirs in our valley." This dish is a true reflection of Chef Kazali's ability to craft a diverse menu while maintaining the classic techniques of France and Asia.

BALLARD

The wee town of Ballard, with a population of about 460 and covering an area of 1.2 square miles, is vivid proof that good things come in small packages. The quaint rural burg is located between Santa Ynez and Los Olivos in the Santa Ynez Valley and is well known for its little red schoolhouse (holding classes since 1883), as well as churches, studios, and an award-winning inn, restaurant, and wine tasting room.

From its beginnings as a Wells Fargo stagecoach station in 1880 and named after the station's proprietor, Ballard has quietly evolved into a wine country destination and is often included in the itineraries of savvy sippers as they hit the valley's wine trails. Putting the town on the twenty-first-century foodie's map is the Ballard Inn and Restaurant, located in the heart of the village. The haute hostelry was named one of America's most romantic inns by American Historic Inns, and chef-owner Budi Kazali's innovative French-Asian fare has earned the restaurant a four-diamond rating.

GRILLED QUAIL WITH THAI-STYLE SALAD

SERVES 4

4 quail, semiboneless
Salt and pepper, to taste

Salad dressing:

1 shallot, minced
1 tablespoon fish sauce
3 limes, juiced
1 tablespoon soy sauce
4 tablespoons canola oil
½ bunch fresh mint, stems removed, chopped
½ bunch fresh cilantro, stems removed, chopped
½ bunch fresh basil, stems removed, chopped
1 jalapeño, seeded and minced
1 teaspoon sugar
Salt and pepper, to taste
½ cup peanuts, shelled and chopped

Salad:

1 pound mesclun
1 carrot, peeled and julienne-cut
¼ red onion, peeled and julienne-cut
1 red pepper, seeded and julienne-cut
2 tomatoes, quartered
1 cucumber, peeled and sliced
½ bunch fresh mint, stems removed, chopped
½ bunch fresh cilantro, stems removed, chopped
½ bunch fresh basil, stems removed, chopped
1 bunch green onions, chopped

Season quail with salt and pepper. Grill the quail over medium-high heat (outdoor barbecue or gas grill) until cooked through, about 3 minutes per side. Remove from heat and set aside.

To make the salad dressing: In a bowl combine the shallot, fish sauce, lime juice, and soy sauce. Slowly whisk in the canola oil. Add the mint, cilantro, basil, jalapeño, and sugar. Mix well. Season with salt and pepper to taste. Reserve the peanuts.

To make the salad: In a salad bowl, combine the mesclun, carrot, red onion, red pepper, tomatoes, cucumber, mint, cilantro, basil and green onion. Toss well to combine.

To serve: Toss the salad with the dressing. Add the peanuts and toss briefly. Divide salad evenly among 4 plates, placing one quail on top of each salad to serve.

Pan-Seared Duck Breast with Sweet Potato Puree & Cherry Pinot Noir Sauce

SERVES 4

4 duck breast halves (8–9 ounces each), skin on

4 sprigs fresh thyme

2 garlic cloves, peeled and chopped

Cherry Pinot Noir sauce:

3 tablespoons dried cherries

1 tablespoon raisins

3 tablespoons brandy

2 shallots, minced

2 garlic cloves, minced

2 tablespoons butter, divided

1 cup Pinot Noir

¼ cup balsamic vinegar

1 cup chicken stock

1 cup beef stock

Salt and freshly ground black pepper, to taste

Sweet potato puree:

1 pound sweet potatoes, peeled and
    cut into 3-inch pieces

½ cup cream

2 garlic cloves, minced

2 tablespoons butter

Salt and freshly ground black pepper, to taste

Score the skin of the duck breasts in a crosshatch pattern. Trim any excess fat. Rub the duck breasts with thyme and garlic, and marinate overnight in the refrigerator.

To make the cherry Pinot Noir sauce: Soak the cherries and raisins in brandy until soft and plump. Strain, reserving the brandy. Sauté the shallots and garlic in 1 tablespoon butter in a sauté pan over medium heat. Add the cherries and raisins. Deglaze the pan with the reserved brandy. Reduce until the pan is nearly dry. Add

the Pinot Noir, and reduce again until nearly dry. Add the balsamic vinegar, reducing until syrupy. Add the chicken and beef stock and reduce until the sauce thickens enough to coat the back of a spoon. Finish with the remaining tablespoon of butter, and season with salt and pepper. Keep warm.

To make the sweet potato puree: Boil the sweet potatoes in salted water until soft. Strain and mash or puree the potatoes. While the potatoes cook, warm the cream and garlic in a saucepan over medium heat. Simmer to reduce to ¼ cup. Add the cream mixture to the pureed sweet potatoes. Add the butter and season with salt and pepper.

Preheat the oven to 400°F.

Sear the duck breasts, skin side down, in an ovenproof sauté pan over medium-high heat, until some of the fat is rendered and the skin is golden brown. Turn and place in the pan in the oven. Cook for 8 minutes for medium rare, or until desired doneness. Remove from heat, and allow the duck to rest for 5 minutes.

Arrange the duck breasts on individual serving plates, top with the cherry Pinot Noir sauce, and serve with a side of sweet potato puree.

Grilled Australian Rack of Lamb with Potato Artichoke Hash & Star Anise Demi-Glace

SERVES 4

Star anise demi-glace:

4 medium shallots, chopped

1 garlic clove, minced

2 tablespoons canola oil

2 cups red wine (Cabernet Sauvignon or Syrah)

2 cups beef stock

1 cup chicken stock

1 star anise

Salt and pepper, to taste

Potato artichoke hash:

2 cups diced Yukon Gold potatoes

1 cup diced sweet potatoes

2 cups diced artichoke pieces, green outer
    leaves and centers removed

3 tablespoons canola oil

1 tablespoon minced garlic

1 tablespoon minced fresh ginger

1 cup diced red bell pepper

1 cup diced yellow onion

Salt and pepper, to taste

2 bunches arugula leaves

4 racks of lamb (10–12 ounces each),
    trimmed of all fat

To make the demi-glace: Sauté the shallots and garlic with the canola oil over medium heat. Deglaze the pan with red wine. Simmer until the liquid is reduced by two-thirds. Add the beef and chicken stock and star anise. Reduce until the sauce coats the back of a spoon. Add salt and pepper to taste. Strain sauce and set aside.

To make the hash: Boil the potatoes and sweet potatoes in salted water until cooked but still firm. Set aside to cool. In a large skillet over medium heat, sauté the artichokes in canola oil until cooked through, stirring frequently, about 10 to 15 minutes. Add the garlic, ginger, red pepper, and onion, and sauté 2 minutes to brown the garlic. Add the blanched potatoes and sweet potatoes and salt and pepper to taste. Continue to sauté until the potatoes are cooked through and begin to brown. Add the arugula last, cooking just long enough to wilt the leaves.

To cook the lamb: Grill the lamb over medium-high heat (outdoor barbecue or gas grill). Grill 6 minutes on the bone side, then turn and grill 4 minutes on the meat side. Remove from heat and let rest for 2 minutes before serving.

To serve: Divide the potato artichoke hash among 4 serving plates. Top each with a rack of lamb, and spoon the sauce over the lamb and hash. Serve immediately.

Santa Barbara County has taken off as a world-class wine producer and red-hot touring and tasting destination. Just about 40 minutes from the town of Santa Barbara, the Santa Ynez Valley is one of four distinct American Viticultural Areas (AVA)—also known as wine appellations—in Santa Barbara County's wine country. The others are Santa Maria Valley, Santa Rita Hills, and Happy Canyon of Santa Barbara. Over 23,000 acres of vineyards in the county produce more than a million cases of wine annually—including the big three of Chardonnay, Pinot Noir, and Syrah, but also superb Riesling, Sauvignon Blanc, Pinot Grigio, Cabernet Sauvignon, Viognier, and dozens of other varietals.

The unusual east-west orientation of the area's coastal mountain ranges creates valleys that funnel cool Pacific Ocean air and fog inland during the late afternoon and evening. Hot sunny days and cool nights are an ideal combination for thriving wine grapes.

Sippers can opt to hit three scenic wine trails, stopping at wineries along the way, or head into towns such as Los Olivos and Solvang, which offer dozens of tasting rooms within steps of one another.

Brothers Restaurant—
Sides Hardware and Shoes

2375 Alamo Pintado Avenue, Los Olivos
(805) 688-4820
www.brothersrestaurant.com
Owners: Jeff and Matt Nichols

After a long, successful stint operating Mattei's Tavern (the celebrated restaurant that was once a former stagecoach stop), Jeff and Matt Nichols have returned to Los Olivos.

The Nichols brothers continue to serve delicious country fare—which now includes breakfast—at their exciting new eatery, Sides Hardware and Shoes, a Brothers Restaurant.

"We decided to go back into Los Olivos history and use the original owner (Melburn Sides) and building," says Jeff.

The restaurant interior has been wonderfully restored to reflect a more casual family atmosphere. Like Mattei's Tavern, which included a popular bar and sitting area, Sides Hardware and Shoes is the perfect place to connect with locals while dining on chef favorites, like filet mignon crispy tacos, and sipping one of Matt's famous pink lemonades.

"Our philosophy remains the same, which is to keep a rather simple approach," adds Jeff. "We acquire the best ingredients, nurture them, and serve them at peak performance."

For starters, the spicy fried calamari and tuna tartare served with crisp wonton chips are two culinary winners. So are the thick-cut prime rib, filet mignon, rack of lamb, and even the mouthwatering Kobe burger. The desserts, including the Tahitian vanilla crème brûlée and mud pie with Kahlúa caramel sauce, are also must-haves, thanks to an outstanding pastry chef.

"Visiting our new restaurant is much like attending a wonderful theatrical performance," says Matt. "It is essential for the success of the performance to be consistently great each and every time the curtain goes up." At Sides Hardware and Shoes, you can expect an encore-worthy performance each and every time.

GRILLED FILLET OF PRIME BEEF WITH
STILTON CHEESE & PORT WINE SAUCE

SERVES 4

¼ cup olive oil

2 tablespoons chopped fresh thyme

4 fillets of prime beef (8 ounces each)

Port wine sauce:

1 teaspoon olive oil

6 ounces lean beef scraps, cut into pieces

1 large shallot, sliced

4 whole garlic cloves, peeled

1 small yellow onion, sliced

2 cups port wine

½ cup demi-glace

½ stick (4 tablespoons) unsalted butter,
    cubed and chilled

Kosher salt, to taste

Freshly ground black pepper, to taste

½ cup crumbled Stilton cheese

Caramelized onion and potato gratin:

2 tablespoons olive oil

2 yellow onions, thinly sliced

1 tablespoon kosher salt, plus more to taste

1 teaspoon white pepper, plus more to taste

1 cup heavy cream

6 large Idaho potatoes, peeled

½ cup crème fraîche or sour cream

1½ cups freshly grated Parmesan

Seasonal vegetables (asparagus, green beans,
    baby carrots, snap peas, etc.)

Kosher salt, to taste

Freshly ground black pepper, to taste

In a small bowl, mix together the olive oil and fresh thyme. Rub the olive oil–thyme marinade evenly over all the prime fillet steaks. Refrigerate for 1 hour or overnight.

To make the port wine sauce: Place a saucepan over high heat. When hot, add the olive oil and then the beef. Allow the beef to sear and caramelize for 6–8 minutes, stirring occasionally. Add the shallot, garlic, and onion and stir to incorporate with the beef. Continue to cook over medium-high heat for another 6–8 minutes, until well caramelized. During this period of caramelizing, control your heat, being careful not to burn the vegetables.

Add the port wine, and reduce the heat to medium. (Caution: cooking over gas with alcohol may cause flare-ups.) Allow the wine to simmer until the liquid is reduced by two-thirds. Add the demi-glace and continue to reduce until the mixture is of sauce consistency, about 1 cup of liquid total.

When the sauce is finished cooking, remove from the heat and strain through a fine sieve into a clean saucepan. Using a ladle or a spoon, push down firmly on the caramelized meat-vegetable mixture, extracting all the juices. Place the saucepan over medium heat and bring the sauce to a simmer. Reduce to sauce consistency (the sauce will coat the back of a spoon). Whisk in the cubed butter. Adjust the seasoning with salt and pepper. Set sauce aside and keep warm. Just before serving, add the crumbled Stilton cheese.

To make the caramelized onion and potato gratin: Heat a large sauté pan over medium heat. Once the pan is hot, add the olive oil and sliced onions. Stir the onions to coat with the olive oil.

Lightly season the onion mixture with salt and white pepper. Stir occasionally, and adjust the heat source as needed, making sure not to burn the onions. If the onions start to stick or burn, add 2 tablespoons water to cool the hot spot and loosen the onions from the pan. Continue to cook the onions until caramelized, about 30 minutes. Transfer to a bowl, cool, and set aside.

Preheat the oven to 400°F. Place the cream in a large bowl and season it with 1 tablespoon kosher salt and 1 teaspoon white pepper. Mix thoroughly. Using a mandoline, slice the potatoes lengthwise into long ⅛-inch-thick slices. Using your hands, toss the sliced potatoes in the seasoned cream to coat.

Lightly grease an 8 x 8-inch baking dish with butter. Make one layer of potatoes in the bottom, slightly overlapping the edges. Repeat two times, making three full layers. After the third layer, evenly disperse the caramelized onions over the top. Finish with 2 or 3 more layers of potatoes.

Use your hands to press on the layers, taking note of how high the cream rises. The cream should fill the pan almost to the top of the pressed layers of potatoes. Remove any excess, or add more seasoned cream if necessary.

Cover the dish with a sheet of aluminum foil. Bake for 1½–2 hours. Test for doneness by pulling back the covering and inserting a paring knife; the potatoes are fully cooked when the paring knife meets no resistance.

To finish the gratin, turn on the broiler. Using a spoon, spread the crème fraîche evenly over the potatoes. Using your hands, spread the grated Parmesan evenly over the crème fraîche. Place the potatoes under the broiler. Watching closely, cook until the Parmesan has melted and is a light golden brown. Turn off broiler and keep potatoes warm in a 200°F oven.

To make the seasonal vegetables: Fill a large stockpot with salted water. Place the pot over high heat and bring the water to a boil. In a bowl, prepare an ice bath. Cook each type of vegetable separately until al dente. Test the vegetable by removing one piece, plunging it into the ice bath, and tasting. If it is al dente, immediately remove all of the vegetables from the boiling water and transfer them into the ice bath. Once the vegetables are thoroughly chilled, remove them from the ice bath and set aside.

To cook the fillets: Preheat a grill to high heat. Season the steaks with salt and black pepper. Grill the steaks until medium rare, or to your preference. Remove from heat.

To serve: Plate the caramelized onion potato gratin and seasonal vegetables. Evenly spoon the Stilton cheese port wine sauce onto the plates. Arrange the grilled fillet of prime beef steaks onto the plate. Serve immediately.

PINOT NOIR–BRAISED SHORT RIBS

SERVES 6

6 short ribs (1 pound each), bone-in
Kosher salt, to taste
Freshly ground black pepper, to taste
Olive oil, as needed
1 medium yellow onion, roughly chopped
1 celery stalk, roughly chopped
1 carrot, roughly chopped
6 whole garlic cloves, peeled
2 cups red wine (Pinot Noir)
2 cups chicken stock
½ cup demi-glace
4 or 5 springs fresh thyme
12–16 whole fingerling potatoes, skin on
½ stick (4 tablespoons) unsalted butter
18 baby carrots

Preheat the oven to 350°F.

Season the ribs liberally with salt and pepper. Heat a large braising pan over high heat. When the pan is hot, add enough olive oil to just cover the bottom. Sear the ribs until they are a dark golden brown on all sides. Remove the ribs from the pan and set aside.

Drain any excess liquid from the pan (but do not clean the bottom). Return the pan to medium heat and add 1 tablespoon of olive oil and the onion, celery, carrot, and garlic. Cook the vegetables until they are lightly caramelized. Add the red wine and let simmer for 10 minutes. Add the chicken stock and demi-glace and bring to a boil. Let simmer for another 10 minutes. Add the short ribs back to the pan, along with the sprigs of thyme. Cover the pan and transfer into the oven for 2 hours. After 2 hours, carefully open the lid and arrange the fingerling potatoes on top. Replace the lid and continue to cook for another 1½–2 hours, or until the short ribs are tender.

Remove the potatoes and short ribs from the pot. Strain the liquid through a fine sieve into a saucepan and skim the liquid to remove the fat. Over medium heat, reduce the liquid by half. Whisk in the butter and remove sauce from heat.

Fill a large stockpot with water and season with salt. Place the pot over high heat and bring the water to a boil. In a bowl, prepare an ice bath. Add the carrots. Cook until al dente. Test the carrots by removing one piece, plunging it into the ice bath, and tasting. If the carrot is cooked al dente, immediately remove all of the carrots from the boiling water and transfer into the ice bath. Once the carrots are thoroughly chilled, remove them from the ice bath and set aside.

Divide the potatoes and carrots among serving plates. Place one short rib onto each plate. Coat the ribs with sauce, letting the sauce run down the short ribs onto the plate. Serve immediately.

Roasted Chicken Breast with Herb–Goat Cheese Stuffing & Thyme Jus

SERVES 6

Herb–goat cheese stuffing:

12 ounces goat cheese
¼ cup chopped fresh thyme

Chicken:

6 chicken breasts (10–12 ounces each),
    skin-on, wing bone attached
¼ cup olive oil
2 tablespoons chopped fresh thyme
Kosher salt, to taste
Black pepper, to taste
Olive oil, for cooking

Thyme jus (makes about 1 cup):

1 chicken carcass (or bones from 1 chicken)
1 celery stalk, roughly chopped
1 carrot, roughly chopped
1 yellow onion, roughly chopped
½ stick unsalted butter, cubed and chilled
4 sprigs fresh thyme, chopped
Kosher salt, to taste
Black pepper, to taste

To make the herb–goat cheese stuffing:
Combine the goat cheese and thyme in a small
mixing bowl. Mix thoroughly and divide into 6
equal portions.

Rinse the chicken breasts under cold water and
dry using paper towels. Trim away any excessive
skin and fat from each chicken breast. Near the
wing bone, use your index finger to make a small
opening under the skin. Run your finger between
the skin and breast meat to make a pocket. Fill
the pocket with the herb–goat cheese stuffing.
Use your fingers to smooth out the stuffed
chicken breast, creating a thin, even layer of
stuffing beneath the skin.

In a small bowl, combine the ¼ cup olive oil and
fresh thyme. Rub the olive oil–thyme marinade
evenly over all the chicken breasts. Refrigerate
for 1 hour or overnight.

To make the thyme jus: Rinse the chicken bones
under cold running water, removing any blood
and remaining organ pieces. Place the bones
into a large stockpot and cook over medium
heat. Stirring occasionally, simmer the bones
until golden brown. (Note: Do not overbrown the
chicken bones, or the jus will taste bitter.) Add
the celery, carrot, and onion to the stockpot
and continue to sear until the vegetables are
golden brown. Add just enough water to cover
the chicken bones and vegetables. Simmer for
1 hour. Using a fine sieve, strain the browned
chicken stock into a clean saucepan. Continue
to simmer the strained stock over medium heat,
reducing and concentrating the stock to 1 cup.
To finish the thyme jus, over low heat, whisk in the
butter and thyme. Taste and adjust the seasoning
with salt and pepper.

Preheat the oven to 425°F.

To cook the chicken: Season the stuffed chicken breasts with salt and black pepper. Heat a large sauté pan over medium-high heat. When the sauté pan is hot, add some olive oil and sauté two chicken breasts at a time, skin-side down. Cook until the skin is golden brown. Turn the breasts over and cook for 2 minutes, then transfer them to a baking sheet. Repeat until all chicken breasts are seared. Place the baking sheet in the oven and bake until the chicken is cooked through, 18 to 20 minutes. Remove from the oven.

To serve: Spoon some mashed potatoes onto the plates. Distribute some seasonal vegetables or spinach among the plates. Plate the chicken breasts and sauce the chicken breast with the thyme jus. Serve immediately.

CELEBRITY VISITS

Santa Barbara's glittery ties to Hollywood go way back. Between 1912 and 1919, Flying A Studios produced more than 1,200 films, many of them Westerns, in Santa Barbara County. The region has continued to take its turn in the spotlight, in films from *Sunset Boulevard* (1950), starring Gloria Swanson, to *It's Complicated* (2009) with Meryl Streep and Alec Baldwin, which was filmed at the 1920s-era Spanish Colonial El Paseo, as well as the Santa Barbara County Courthouse.

A popular spot for A-listers in their off-hours, too, Santa Barbara has played host to old-time movie stars, such as Rock Hudson and Lana Turner, and swarms of current celebs like Brad Pitt, Gwyneth Paltrow, and Michelle Pfeiffer. The annual Santa Barbara International Film Festival draws some of the hottest names in Hollywood, from Sandra Bullock and Colin Firth to Angelina Jolie and George Clooney.

Also seen soaking up the stunning Santa Barbara scenery have been buzz-worthy politicians from Barack Obama to Bill Clinton, who visited while in office, jogging and joining in a beach volleyball game and noshing at the Nugget in Summerland.

Ca'Dario Ristorante

37 East Victoria Street, Santa Barbara
(805) 884-9419
www.cadario.net
Owner: Dario Furlati

Ca'Dario Ristorante is an intimate restaurant just off State Street in Santa Barbara, and it has proved a locals' favorite since opening in 1997.

Ca'Dario is a lively and charming eatery with mahogany walls and small, quaint tables dressed in white tablecloths, a scene reminiscent of an Italian neighborhood trattoria. The walls are decorated with black and white photos of well-known Italians, and the background music is mixed from Frank Sinatra classics and popular Italian tunes. There is a small bar where you can enjoy a cocktail or glass of wine before dining; regulars might pull up a bar stool and enjoy dinner while watching the hustle and bustle of the kitchen and serving staff.

The restaurant's colorful executive chef and owner, Dario Furlati, oversees the top-rated food. Hailing from Il Lago di Como, which is in northern Italy near Milan, he learned kitchen basics from his grandmothers from Lake Como and the Veneto region. Dario has been in kitchens nearly all his life, and he brings old-world favorites such as osso bucco and tagliatelle bolognese to life in a traditional ristorante. The cozy dining experience is enhanced by Dario's staff, which he lovingly refers to as his family.

The emphasis is on fresh, local produce from farmers' markets and organic meat and fish. As for the pasta, the ravioli with sage and butter is a local favorite. Risotto, fish, and meat specials change daily. An extensive wine list features Italian and Californian wines, while the cocktail menu boasts traditional Italian offerings and more.

PAN-ROASTED CHICKEN BREAST

SERVES 4

4 chicken breasts (10 ounces each),
  boneless with skin on
Salt and white pepper, to taste
4 tablespoons olive oil
1 tablespoon minced shallot
1 tablespoon minced garlic
6 baby artichokes, cut in half
2 cups button mushrooms
½ cup white wine
Juice of 1 lemon
1 cup chicken stock
4 whole lemon slices
Italian parsley sprigs, for garnish

Preheat the oven to 400°F.

Sprinkle the chicken with salt and pepper.

Heat the oil in an ovenproof sauté pan over medium heat. Add the chicken and brown skin side first. Turn the chicken and add the shallots, garlic, artichokes halves, and mushrooms. Cook for another 3 or 4 minutes. Add white wine, and let evaporate. Add the lemon juice and chicken stock. Place the lemon slices on top of the chicken and finish the breasts by transferring the pan to the preheated oven for 20 minutes.

Assemble the dish by placing chicken on the plate, followed by the artichokes and mushroom sauce. Garnish with the fresh parsley sprigs.

ROASTED RACK OF LAMB

SERVES 2

1 rack of lamb (14–16 ounces)
Salt and black pepper, to taste
2 tablespoons olive oil
6 garlic cloves, sliced
2 fresh rosemary sprigs
4 fresh sage leaves
2 tablespoons butter

Preheat the oven to 400°F. Sprinkle the lamb rack with salt and pepper.

Heat the oil in an ovenproof sauté pan over high heat. Add the rack of lamb and sear until brown. Turn the lamb, and add the garlic, rosemary, sage, and butter. Cook the lamb in the preheated oven for 12 minutes (for medium rare).

Assemble the dish by cutting the lamb in four sections. Place each piece of lamb on a plate and add the garlic and herb sauce. Serve with your favorite vegetable.

Quail with Sausage & Polenta

SERVES 4

1 pound instant cornmeal (available at specialty
    Italian markets)

4 quails, cleaned and rinsed

Salt and freshly ground black pepper, to taste

6 ounces Italian sausage (1½ ounces per serving),
    crumbled

2 tablespoons olive oil

1 tablespoon minced shallots

1 tablespoon minced garlic

1 cup chopped fresh porcini mushrooms

1 cup red wine

1 cup chicken stock

2 cups spinach

½ tablespoon olive oil

1 clove fresh garlic, peeled and minced

4 fresh rosemary sprigs

To make the polenta: Boil 2 quarts of salted water. Slowly add the cornmeal to the water using a whisk. Cook, stirring, for 10 minutes over low heat. Remove and keep warm.

Preheat the oven to 400°F. Sprinkle the quails inside and out with salt and pepper. Stuff the quail cavities with the Italian sausage.

Heat the olive oil in a large ovenproof sauté pan over medium heat. Add the quails and brown the breast side first. Turn the quails and add the shallots, garlic, and mushrooms. Continue to cook over medium heat for 3–4 minutes. Add the red wine and reduce until pan is almost dry. Add the chicken stock and stir. Finish the quails by removing the pan from the heat and transferring it to the preheated oven for 10–12 minutes, or until the quail and sausage are cooked through but not dry.

To sauté the spinach: Add the olive oil and garlic to a large fry pan or wok over medium-high heat. Add the spinach leaves and toss frequently until leaves are wilted. Remove from heat.

Serve the polenta on individual serving plates. Top with the spinach. Place a quail on top of the spinach and ladle the porcini mushroom sauce on the sides of the dish. Garnish with a rosemary sprig.

SEAGRASS RESTAURANT

30 EAST ORTEGA STREET, SANTA BARBARA
(805) 963-1012
WWW.SEAGRASSRESTAURANT.COM
OWNERS: THE PEREZ FAMILY

If you're looking for a classy, upscale restaurant that cares about the environment and pays homage to farmers, fishermen, and winemakers who support sustainability while also providing the freshest, highest quality organic ingredients to customers, stop in and enjoy a wonderful coastal meal at Seagrass Restaurant, located just off State Street and within walking distance of the beach.

When offered finely aged meats from Sonoma, fresh crisp produce and vegetables from Santa Barbara farmers' markets, and sustainable seafood fresh from the Pacific, you'll have a difficult time deciding what to order. Heirloom tomato salad, sautéed black cod, slow braised short ribs (the garlicky version is featured here), and Muscovy duck confit are just a few delicious samples from the menu created by chef extraordinaire Robert Perez.

The same can be said about the extensive wine list, which is perfectly paired with the succulent dishes and showcases varietals from some of the best wineries in Santa Barbara County.

The Seagrass ambience—a blend of romantic and tropical with ocean accents—is equally intoxicating as the fabulous food. Among the plantation shutters, soft white textures, vibrant paintings, and comfortable chairs, you'll feel you're being served a home-cooked meal inside a cozy beachfront cottage. There's outdoor seating, too, and if you like dining in shorts and flip-flops, the restaurant offers "Laid Back Sundays" for those who prefer to come as they are.

Seagrass Restaurant is Zagat-rated as the number-one Santa Barbara restaurant, and it received 2011's Award of Excellence from *Wine Spectator.*

BRAISED GARLICKY SHORT RIBS

SERVES 4

Red wine–rosemary syrup:

3 cups dry red wine, good quality
½ cup red wine vinegar
½ cup sugar
1 sprig fresh rosemary

4 beef short ribs (14–16 ounces each, 2 inches thick)
Sea salt and freshly ground black pepper, to taste
½ stick (4 tablespoons) unsalted butter
4 tablespoons olive oil
1 medium onion, peeled and diced
1 celery stalk, diced
1 carrot, peeled and diced
20 garlic cloves
2 tablespoons tomato paste
1 sprig fresh thyme
2 bay leaves
3 cups red wine
1 cup veal stock
½ cup water
4 tablespoons cold butter, to finish sauce

Garnish:

2 tablespoons butter
1 large carrot, peeled and sliced
2 ribs celery, sliced
1 ounce pearl onions, blanched and peeled
20 garlic cloves, peeled and sauteed

To make the red wine–rosemary syrup: Combine the red wine, vinegar, sugar, and rosemary in a heavy-bottomed pot and reduce to a syrup-like consistency. Remove from heat and keep warm.

Preheat the oven to 350°F. Season short ribs with sea salt and pepper. Sauté the ribs in a skillet over high heat with the butter and olive oil until the ribs are golden brown. Remove the ribs from the skillet, and place in a roasting pan. Add the onion, celery, carrot, and garlic to the skillet and sauté on high heat until the vegetables have caramelized. Add the tomato paste and sauté to remove the acidity. Add the thyme and bay leaves and deglaze the pan with red wine, reducing until it is almost dry.

Add the stock and water, and bring to a boil. Pour the vegetables and sauce over the short ribs, cover with aluminum foil, and braise in the oven for approximately 3 hours, or until ribs are tender.

Remove ribs from the pan, cover, and keep warm. Strain the sauce through a fine mesh strainer into a saucepan, bring to a boil, and skim off any impurities. Check the seasoning. Reduce the sauce to the desired consistency and add the red wine–rosemary syrup. Whisk in the cold butter. Warm the vegetable garnish with butter. Arrange the ribs on the plate, spoon the sauce over the ribs, spoon the vegetables onto the plate, and serve.

TRATTORIA ULIVETO

285 SOUTH BROADWAY, OLD ORCUTT
(805) 934-4546
WWW.TRATTORIAULIVETO.COM
OWNERS: ALFONSO CURTI AND JIM SPALLINO

Those who crave authentic Italian food in an energetic setting often make a reservation at Trattoria Grappolo in Santa Ynez. But did you know that Alfonso Curti, ex-chef at brother Leonardo's Trattoria Grappolo, now is executive chef at his own trattoria? Head twenty minutes north from Santa Ynez, and you'll enter the little town of Orcutt. Find your way into Old Orcutt, where Trattoria Uliveto is situated on the quiet street of South Broadway. The restaurant packs in a full house virtually every night, particularly on weekends.

"I enjoy creating specials that reflect the many regions of Italy, while also making sure to incorporate fresh California ingredients," says Alfonso. "Our guests like experiencing both elements when they come in, so we always promise to deliver."

From the sliced New York steak fanned on a bed of fresh arugula (featured here) to the Osso Bucco alla Milanese (also featured), the combination of rustic Italian cuisine with a central California flare is what makes Trattoria Uliveto an exotic destination—passports not required.

All the seats in the house make for great dining. The front dining room can get a little congested, so if you don't like crowds, request a table in the back, where there's more elbow room and the ambience feels more romantic. You can also sit at the rear counter where the pizzas are made, if you prefer marveling at a pizza chef's handiwork as you dine. And don't forget to order one of the restaurant's fabulous desserts before you depart.

"I believe in offering a collection of rustic desserts that are informal and unpretentious," adds Alfonso. "Our desserts reflect the simplicity and casualness found at our restaurant."

SLICED NEW YORK STEAK OVER ARUGULA WITH SHAVED PARMESAN

SERVES 4

4 (10- to 12-ounce) New York steaks
¼ cup extra-virgin olive oil
3 cups arugula
½ cup cherry tomatoes, halved

Olive oil, to taste
Sea salt and freshly cracked black pepper, to taste
Parmesan cheese, shaved, for garnish
2 lemons, cut in wedges, for garnish

Rub each steak with olive oil. Grill the steaks under the broiler or on an outdoor grill until medium rare (or to your liking) and let rest for 10 minutes.

Mound a handful of arugula in the center of each serving plate. Add the tomatoes and drizzle with olive oil. Slice the steak into thin strips and arrange over the arugula. Sprinkle salt and pepper over the top. Top with Parmesan, drizzle with olive oil once more, and serve immediately with the lemon wedges.

Osso Bucco alla Milanese

SERVES 4

4 veal shanks (2½ inches thick)
All-purpose flour, for dusting
4 pinches sea salt
4 tablespoons olive oil
1 medium yellow onion (about 6 ounces),
    cut into ½-inch pieces
1 carrot, cut into ½-inch pieces
1 celery stalk, cut into ½-inch pieces
2 tablespoons chopped fresh rosemary
2 tablespoons chopped fresh sage
2 bay leaves
3 cups chicken stock
½ cup plum tomatoes, chopped

Preheat the oven to 350°F.

Dust the veal shanks with flour and season with salt. Coat a roasting pan with the olive oil and heat on the stovetop over high heat. When hot, arrange the veal shanks in the pan, but do not overcrowd. Brown the veal on both sides, about 5 minutes per side.

Remove the veal shanks from the pan and add the onion, carrot, celery, rosemary, sage, and bay leaves. Reduce the heat to low and cook on the stovetop for about 10 minutes. Add the chicken stock and tomatoes. Bring to a boil. Return the veal shank to the pan and cover. Cook in the oven for 3 hours, or until the shanks are tender.

Serve with a side of risotto or mashed potatoes.

Sautéed Veal Chop with Morel Mushrooms & Brandy

SERVES 4

¼ cup olive oil
4 (10-ounce) veal chops
Salt and freshly ground black pepper, to taste
¼ cup brandy
1 cup sliced morel mushrooms
2 tablespoons Dijon mustard
2 cups heavy cream
1 small bunch fresh thyme, stems removed, chopped
½ cup chicken stock
1 tablespoon truffle oil

In a sauté pan over medium heat, heat the olive oil. Add the veal chops and cook on each side, about 5 minutes per side. Add the salt and pepper, brandy, mushrooms, mustard, cream, thyme, and chicken stock. Continue cooking until the veal is cooked through and the sauce is creamy.

Remove from heat and serve the veal chops on individual plates. Spoon the sauce over the top and drizzle with truffle oil just before serving.

TOP TEN SANTA BARBARA ADVENTURES

1. ART WALKS

Whether you're strolling through the eclectic galleries on State Street, in the historic La Arcada courtyard, or up north in pastoral Los Olivos, you will discover many local artists exhibiting their work. From landscapes and seascapes to portraits and sculptures of cowboys and California pioneers, there are a plethora of galleries offering a variety of media for art lovers to enjoy. If your taste tends toward Picasso and Van Gogh, visit the Santa Barbara Museum of Art for amazing exhibitions and collections.

2. BEACH COMBING

There's no shortage of beautiful beaches in Santa Barbara. Aside from the usual tanning, jogging, and sporting activities on the sand, like beach volleyball, some of the area's most picturesque beaches are home to incredible tide pools and flourishing marine life that's ready for discovery. For nature enthusiasts seeking that perfect seashell or swarming tide pool, visit the golden beaches at Arroyo Burro, Carpinteria, Goleta, Guadalupe, Jalama, Leadbetter, Lookout Park, and Ocean Beach.

3. EXPLORING THE CHANNEL ISLANDS

Feeling landlocked? Ready to explore the islands off the coast, just like early explorers did centuries ago? Catch a boat that will ferry you to the famous Channel Islands located off the coast of Santa Barbara. Whether it's just for the day, or an overnight camping trip, the "local" islands—Anacapa and Santa Cruz—are the most popular and will provide you with endless stimulation. If you'd like to venture further, sail to the outer islands of Santa Rosa, San Miguel (you'll need a permit to disembark here), and Santa Barbara Island. Sometimes the crossing from Santa Barbara to the Channel Islands can get choppy, so don't forget the Dramamine.

4. HIKING

Not all activities in Santa Barbara revolve around or near the water. Lace up your hiking boots to experience some of the most incredible hiking and backpacking trails in central California's interior. There are "front country" hikes for those who would like to be rewarded with breathtaking views overlooking Santa Barbara, and there are "back country" hikes for serious adventurers who would rather be led away from town and deep into the Los Padres National Forest.

5. FISHING

Santa Barbara is an angler's paradise. If you enjoy fly and freshwater fishing, there are many lakes and rivers in which to try your luck. Nearby Lake Cachuma is a productive fishery that yields plenty of good-sized largemouth bass and rainbow trout. For saltwater anglers, surf fishing is quite popular along many of the beaches, as is deep-sea fishing. Many of the fishing charters depart from the Santa Barbara Harbor, so head to the docks for your chance to land a trophy lingcod, rockfish, halibut, or sea bass.

6. SAILING

If you prefer to captain a boat yourself, rent a small craft at the Santa Barbara Sailing Center and cruise through the historic and tranquil harbor. For those who would rather grace the bow, sipping a chilled

Chardonnay while someone else takes the helm, there are many skippered charters available. Sunset cruises are also popular, so visit the waterfront and choose from a variety of sailing options—including classes—depending on your skill or mood.

7. SURFING

It's not Hawaii's North Shore, but Santa Barbara's stunning coastline does produce some worthy waves for those eager to throw on a pair of board shorts, wax up, and head into the surf. Popular surf sites include Goleta and Rincon. Beginners should check out Leadbetter Point. Remember, Santa Barbara is a beach town, so there are ample surf shops at which to inquire about where to go, rent a short or long board, or grab that last-minute accessory.

8. WHALE WATCHING

Santa Barbara's coastline is perfectly situated on the migration map for whales. From February through April, gray whales arrive in healthy numbers. Later in the year, from May through September, blue whales, humpbacks and minke whales make their appearance. Stroll down to the harbor and board a whale watching boat. The boats patrol close to shore, and while you're waiting for a whale, there's a good chance you'll spot dolphins, seals, and sea lions.

9. WINE TASTING

See the movie *Sideways*? It was filmed in the heart of Santa Barbara wine country. There are a few tasting rooms in downtown Santa Barbara, but aficionados seeking the ultimate wine experience head north to the bucolic town of Los Olivos. There are guided and self-guided tours, as well as an endless array of tasting rooms showcasing the best central California has to offer. Many say the Santa Barbara County wine tasting experience is what Napa used to be many years ago, when you were able to chat with the winemaker and taste right from the barrel.

10. ZOO ANIMAL FUN

Imagine a zoo that overlooks the sparkling Pacific Ocean. No wonder many call the Santa Barbara Zoo one of the most beautiful zoos in the world. Nestled on thirty acres, this prized ocean-view property is home to more than 500 animals. Spend a day exploring the many natural exhibits, which include African lions, Asian elephants, gorillas, anteaters, leopards, monkeys, and flamingos. There are also plenty of lush rolling lawns and shady areas to have lunch, picnic, or simply soak up the sun.

Decadent Desserts

Desserts are always the grand finale—the last bite your family and friends will enjoy—so they should make a lasting impression or memory.

Cafe Shell's Shelley Shoemaker, who grew up in the food industry and later created wedding cakes for her parents' restaurant, begins with a marvelous strawberry shortcake and melt-in-your-mouth Bittersweet Chocolate Brownies, two signature sweets that will win over the most finicky of dessert eaters. Coast Restaurant & Bar invites you to try a handcrafted Toffee Cake and a clafouti made with fresh cherries and slivered almonds. Jane Restaurant—sister to the famed Montecito Cafe—showcases a creamy and traditional crème brûlée, followed by a decadent red velvet cake finished with a simple-to-make cream cheese frosting. No need to count calories at this point, as Olio e Limone Ristorante continues building the dessert menu with a delectable pear tart with homemade marzipan and caramel sauce. Renaud's Patisserie & Bistro invites you to try its golden delicious madeleines and the to-die-for Parisien Chocolate Macaroons with Chocolate Garnish. And the Vineyard House emphasizes presentation and a culinary "wow" factor with rum-flamed Macadamia Nut Banana Foster and a prized—and gooey—Molten Chocolate Cake with Dark Cherry Brandy Sauce.

No matter what dessert you choose, each pairs well with a fresh cup of roasted coffee, a hot espresso, a fine aged port, or a glass of Italian limoncello, an iridescent yellow liqueur that's thick and icy cold, with an intense citrus bite.

Café Shell

1112 State Street, Santa Barbara
(805) 965-5742
Owner: Shelley Shoemaker

Turn off the phone, bring the Sunday paper, and enjoy a quintessential Santa Barbara moment under the sunny yellow umbrellas. No hurries, no worries: this is brunch at Café Shell.

For more than twenty years, Santa Barbara locals have enjoyed the restaurant's beautiful outdoor seating in scenic and artistic La Arcada Court. In the heart of it all, the cafe is a welcome respite from your day enjoying State Street. Visit for brunch on one of three outdoor patios and sip tangerine mimosas, white peach Bellinis, and local wines. Alternatively, relax in the sun as you dine on one of the many signature eggs benedict dishes or omelets. Enjoy generous sandwiches made with Santa Barbara's own Shalhoob meats, Our Daily Bread Bakery breads, and local produce. Café Shell makes three soups daily, and the chicken chili topped with melted cheddar cheese and cilantro has an avid local following. Refreshing lemon bars with shortbread crust and delicious espresso drinks will end your meal on a sweet note and fuel you for your day of shopping. As a special treat, Café Shell offers two favorite dessert recipes here—homemade Special-Occasion Shortcakes and Bittersweet Chocolate Brownies.

When in Santa Barbara, look for the cafe's famous outdoor bronze sculptures, especially the turtle fountain for the little ones. The historic architecture by Myron Hunt puts this restaurant on the map of must-sees, so whether it's a picnic lunch for the beach, enjoying parade route seating for Solstice and Fiesta, or a celebratory lunch with friends and family, make this tradition your own.

Bittersweet Chocolate Brownies

MAKES 15 BROWNIES

¾ pound bittersweet chocolate (50 to 60 percent cacao)
3 sticks butter
1 cup cocoa powder
10 eggs
3½ cups sugar
1 cup all-purpose flour

In a saucepan over low heat (or using a double boiler), melt the chocolate and butter until smooth, about 3 minutes. Remove from heat and transfer the melted chocolate and butter to the refrigerator for about 12 minutes. Remove from refrigerator and stir in the cocoa. Return to refrigerator for 8 minutes.

Preheat the oven to 350°F.

In a mixing bowl, whisk the eggs and sugar together until combined. Do not overmix. Remove the chocolate from the refrigerator and add the egg and sugar mixture. Whisk until mixed. Stir in the flour. Pour the chocolate mixture into a greased and floured 12 x 8 x 3-inch baking dish. Place in the refrigerator for 15 minutes.

Bake oven for 36 minutes. Rotate the dish halfway through baking. Remove from oven and let cool. When cool, cut into individual brownies and serve.

SPECIAL-OCCASION SHORTCAKES WITH STRAWBERRIES & WHIPPED CREAM

SERVES 8

4 pints strawberries

1 cup sugar

3 tablespoons orange juice

Shortcakes:

2 cups all-purpose bleached flour,
    plus more for work surface

¾ teaspoon salt

1 tablespoon baking powder

4 tablespoons sugar

1 stick (8 tablespoons) unsalted butter, frozen

1 egg

½ cup heavy cream, plus additional for brushing

1 teaspoon lemon zest

¼ cup coarse sugar, for sprinkling

Whipped Cream (makes about 2 cups):

1 cup heavy cream, chilled

3 tablespoons vanilla syrup

Whole strawberries, for garnish

Hull and slice the strawberries. Transfer one-quarter to a small bowl and slightly crush with a potato masher. Combine all the strawberries with the sugar and orange juice in a large glass or ceramic bowl. Refrigerate for 30 minutes to extract natural juices.

Preheat the oven to 425°F.

To make the shortcakes, mix the flour, salt, baking powder, and sugar in a large bowl. Using the large holes of a box grater, grate the frozen butter into the dry ingredients. Mix the butter to coat with flour. Use a pastry cutter to finish cutting the butter into the flour, until mixture forms pea-size pieces.

In a separate bowl, beat the egg and cream. Add the zest, and then pour into the dry ingredients. Blend with a fork until the mixture holds together. Turn the dough onto a floured work surface and barely knead until it comes together. Pat the dough into a 1-inch-thick circle. Cut 8 dough rounds with a floured biscuit cutter.

Place the dough rounds 1 inch apart on an aluminum baking pan (round is best, but a cookie sheet is also fine). Brush the shortcake rounds with cream and sprinkle with coarse sugar. Bake until golden brown, about 12 minutes.

Cool the rounds on the counter, but serve warm, if possible. You can also reheat the rounds for 3–5 minutes if you choose to serve them later.

The restaurant uses a stainless-steel whipped cream canister, simply inserting the CO_2 charger, cream, and vanilla syrup. The cream pipes beautifully. To whip the cream without one, combine the cream and vanilla and beat on high with a hand mixer or stand mixer just until soft peaks form. (Note: Do not whip cream until stiff; it's always yummier to have soft whipped cream than a grainy butter-like texture.)

To serve, cut open each shortcake and fill with the strawberries and whipped cream. Replace the top and serve with more berry mixture and cream. Garnish the cream with half a strawberry (green top on).

Coast Restaurant & Bar

31 West Carrillo Street, Santa Barbara
(805) 879-9100
WWW.CANARYSANTABARBARA.COM
Owner: The Edward Thomas Collection

Formerly the Hotel Andaluca, Santa Barbara's boutique Canary Hotel, which was inspired by the Canary Islands and central California's coastal beauty, offers stunning accommodations, Spanish decor, and the best rooftop view in town. The world-class hotel, popular with residents for both food and atmosphere, is also home to the popular Coast Restaurant & Bar.

From extravagant Sunday brunches with live jazz, to nightly comfort food entrees such as chicken tortilla soup, day-boat scallops, Dungeness crab cakes, and braised

lamb ravioli coupled with scrumptious cocktails, Coast is the place to unwind and enjoy the perfect meal in a luxurious setting. There are plenty of daily specials and bar food, particularly during happy hour, including the always-popular crispy tacos (your choice of chicken, steak, pork, or snapper) and juicy and savory sliders with skinny french fries.

Desserts at Coast are equally tempting, and such sinful surprises are the perfect ending to a glorious evening. Must-tries are the creamy puddings, fresh orchard crisps and cobblers, and the two treats featured here—a decadent toffee cake topped with caramel, candied nuts, and ice cream, and the traditionally French clafouti finished with a light coating of powdered sugar.

TOFFEE CAKE

SERVES 6–8

1 cup water
1 teaspoon baking soda
11 ounces chopped dates
1½ cups all-purpose flour
2 teaspoons baking powder
Pinch of salt
½ stick (4 tablespoons) unsalted butter
¾ cup packed brown sugar
2 large eggs
½ teaspoon vanilla extract
Caramel sauce, for garnish
Candied nuts, for garnish
Ice cream or whipped cream, for garnish

Preheat the oven to 350°F.

In a small saucepan over high heat, bring the water, baking soda, and chopped dates to a boil. When boiling, remove from heat and set aside to cool.

In a medium bowl, sift together the flour, baking powder, and salt. In the bowl of a stand mixer with paddle attachment, cream the butter and brown sugar together until smooth. Slowly add the eggs and vanilla. When completely mixed, scrape the sides and add the dry ingredients in three equal additions, mixing in each before adding the next. Add the dates and water, and mix well to combine.

Pour the batter into a buttered 9 x 9-inch or 10 x 7-inch baking dish, and place on the center rack in the oven. Bake until a toothpick inserted in the center comes out clean. Depending on the size of the baking dish, it will take 9–15 minutes. Remove from oven and allow to cool.

Serve with caramel sauce, candied nuts, and ice cream or whipped cream.

Clafouti

SERVES 6–8

½ cup pitted fresh cherries
¼ cup slivered almonds
3 eggs
1 cup sugar
1 tablespoon brown sugar
⅛ teaspoon salt
½ cup all-purpose flour, sifted
1 cup whole milk
2 teaspoons Amaretto or ¾ teaspoon almond extract
1½ teaspoons vanilla extract
Powdered sugar, for dusting

Preheat the oven to 350°F.

Butter and lightly flour a 9 x 9-inch or 10 x 7-inch baking dish. Spread the cherries and slivered almonds on the bottom.

In a mixing bowl, combine the eggs, sugars, salt, and flour. Whisk until smooth. Add the milk, Amaretto or almond extract, and vanilla extract. Whisk again until smooth. Pour into the baking dish.

Bake for 40–50 minutes, or until lightly browned. A toothpick inserted into the center should come out clean. Carefully remove the baking dish from the oven (the clafouti will wiggle, which is normal). Place on a wire rack to cool. The clafouti will have puffed up and will deflate while cooling.

When cool, dust with powdered sugar and serve.

JANE RESTAURANT

1311 STATE STREET, SANTA BARBARA
(805) 962-1311
WWW.JANERESTAURANTSB.COM
OWNERS: MARK AND MARGARET HUSTON

Santa Barbara resident Jane Chapman is proud to pay homage to her wonderful grandmother, Jane. That's why she and her parents—Mark and Margaret Huston, owners of the Montecito Cafe—opened a charming restaurant on State Street to serve exceptional food based on family recipes while introducing Grandmother Jane to the rest of the community. Today, Jane's spirit and legacy flourish.

Jane Restaurant, definitely one of the favorite places to dine in town, serves local fish, the finest meats, traditional pasta dishes, and garden-fresh salad bowls both inside amidst the cozy home-style decor (including black-and-white photographs of Grandmother Jane) and outside on the cute balcony.

"We strive to keep our menu prices and wine list reasonable and fair, giving our customers exceptional value for the quality of food, ambiance, and service," say the Hustons. "And we believe service should be fast, complete, and friendly, but not overbearing." Visit the restaurant and you'll often find Jane working the front of the house with her infectious smile. It's definitely a family affair here.

All of the soups, sauces, salad dressings, and hamburger buns are prepared daily from scratch. Same with the delightful desserts, which are handcrafted by the dedicated pastry chef, who uses only the freshest ingredients. Signature dishes at Jane include Papaya and Dungeness Crab Salad, Grilled Salmon on Alder Wood, Grilled Filet Mignon with Mushroom Herb Sauce, and an exceptionally moist Coconut Cake. There is also a children's menu, as well as vegetarian options.

CRÈME BRÛLÉE

SERVES 4

1 quart heavy whipping cream
1 fresh vanilla bean
7 egg yolks, at room temperature
$^2/_3$ cup granulated sugar
$^2/_3$ cup brown sugar, plus extra for caramelizing

Pour the cream into a saucepan. Slice the vanilla bean open and scrape out the inside. Add both the insides and the bean to the cream. Over medium-high heat, bring the cream mixture up to scalding.

Mix the egg yolks and sugars together by hand in a large mixing bowl. Do not overmix.

Slowly add a little of the hot cream to the egg mixture, whisking steadily to avoid cooking the eggs. Continue the process until all the cream is used. Strain the mixture into a pitcher with a fine-mesh strainer.

Preheat the oven to 300°F.

Place the ceramic baking dishes, such as soufflé molds or ramekins, into a large baking pan, such as a casserole or hotel pan. Use a large-enough pan to allow for some space between the baking dishes. Fill each baking dish almost to the top with the custard mix. Then pour water around the outside of the dishes. The water bath should come halfway up the sides of the ramekins.

The baking time will vary; check after 20 minutes by jiggling the custard a bit. The custard should not be liquid inside, but rather jiggling like Jell-O. Don't let the custard boil, as the brûlées will be ruined.

Move the custards into the refrigerator and allow to cool completely, at least 2 hours, and ideally overnight.

To serve, cover the top of the custard with about 1/16 inch of brown sugar and caramelize with a kitchen torch or under a broiler.

Red Velvet Cake

MAKES 1 (12-INCH) CAKE

Cake:

3⅓ cups cake flour

1½ sticks (12 tablespoons) butter, room temperature

2¼ cups sugar

3 large eggs, room temperature

6 tablespoons red food coloring

3 tablespoons unsweetened cocoa

1½ teaspoons vanilla extract

1½ teaspoons salt

1½ cups buttermilk

1½ teaspoons cider vinegar

1½ teaspoons baking soda

Cream cheese frosting:

1½ sticks (12 tablespoons) unsalted butter, softened

10 ounces cream cheese, room temperature

2½ cups powdered sugar

1 tablespoon vanilla

Preheat the oven to 350°F.

Sift the cake flour into a mixing bowl and set aside.

Using a stand mixer with paddle attachment, combine the butter and sugar in the mixing bowl and mix on medium speed until combined. With the mixer running, add the eggs, one at a time.

In a small mixing bowl, whisk together the food coloring, cocoa, and vanilla. Add the mixture to the egg batter. In another small bowl, combine the salt and buttermilk and whisk to combine. Slowly add to the batter, along with the cake flour. In yet another small bowl, whisk together the cider vinegar and baking soda. Add to the batter and mix well, until all the ingredients are combined.

Pour cake batter into three greased cake pans. Bake for 30–40 minutes, and remove from oven. Allow cake to cool before frosting.

To make the cream cheese frosting, mix the butter and cream cheese with an electric mixer on medium speed until smooth. Sift the powdered sugar and add it into the butter and cream cheese in three batches, mixing until smooth. Add the vanilla and mix to combine.

Frost the cake generously with cream cheese frosting and serve.

OLIO E LIMONE RISTORANTE

17 WEST VICTORIA STREET, SANTA BARBARA
(805) 899-2699
WWW.OLIOELIMONE.COM
OWNERS: ALBERTO AND ELAINE MORELLO

On West Victoria Street in downtown Santa Barbara is the Italian trattoria Olio e Limone (meaning "oil and lemon"). Founded by Elaine Morello and husband, chef Alberto Morello, this heralded restaurant is intimate, classy and, although you may find it quiet at times, a sophisticated establishment—perfect for a romantic evening. If you happen to stop by during lunch or prefer a little added excitement anytime, grab a seat at the counter in front of the pizza oven. It's always fun to dine while watching the chefs hurl fresh pizza dough through the air.

At Olio e Limone, you will discover creative pan-Italian cuisine with touches of Sicily, like a finely presented plate of Fiorellini di Melanzane—house-made ravioli filled with roasted eggplant and goat cheese, topped with a fresh tomato and basil sauce and shaved ricotta salata. You can also savor fresh seafood delicacies like the Pesce Spada con Caponata (lightly breaded swordfish fillet with Sicilian ratatouille). Because the food is so good, you'll need a reservation to get a table.

Be sure to take a moment and peruse the tempting dessert menu. At Olio e Limone, the homemade dolci are outstanding, especially the Crostata di Pera con Pasta Reale (pear tart with marzipan and caramel sauce, featured here courtesy of Olio e Limone Ristorante and Alberto and Elaine Morello).

DESSERTS IN A SICILIAN HOME

In most Sicilian homes, a bowl of fruit bobbing in ice water is placed on the table after a meal. The most common fruits included are apricots, peaches, oranges, plums, blood oranges, Mandarin tangerines, cherries, prickly pears, figs, dates, and strawberries. Sweets are eaten at any time of the day, not typically as a dessert course at the end of a meal. The single most famous Sicilian dessert is probably cannoli, a tube of fried pastry filled with fresh sheep ricotta, sugar, candied orange peel, and pistachios. Cassata, a sponge cake decorated with fruit—the queen of Sicilian dessert—is the crowning glory of the Easter table.

There are so many Sicilian treats—*sfince* (Italian doughnuts), *zeppole* (deep-fried dough), *torrone* (almond candy), *cucuzata* (candied squash), granita (Italian ice, like sorbet), jasmine sorbet—it is hard to choose. One that we love in particular is *pasta reale*, literally translated as "royal dough." We know it better as marzipan.

Religion and confectionary have gone hand in hand for centuries in Sicily. Sequestered convent nuns found a creative outlet in the preparation of special *dolci*. Marzipan was first fashioned into shapes by nuns at the convent of the church of Martorana in Palermo. They molded the marzipan into fruit shapes to hang on bare branches of the trees in their garden in honor of visiting bishops. The expert confectioners of Sicily still sculpt marzipan into fruit shapes; once the fantastic marzipan sculptures are dry, they are colored to resemble real fruit. Marzipan may also be used to enrich different pastries. Our favorite example of this is Olio e Limone's pear tart. Chef Alberto and our Italian neighbor cut the molds we use to shape the dough by hand out of metal.

Courtesy of Olio e Limone Ristorante and Alberto and Elaine Morello

Pear Tart with Marzipan & Caramel Sauce

SERVES 6

Pears:

6 firm but ripe pears (Bartlett or Comice)
¾ bottle white wine
½ gallon water
1 stick cinnamon
2 cups sugar
Zest and juice of 1 lemon
1 fresh vanilla bean

Marzipan:

9 ounces almond powder
9 ounces sugar
Pinch of powdered vanilla
3 drops orange blossom water
2 egg whites

Puff pastry:

21 x 10-inch sheet frozen puff pastry dough
2 eggs, beaten

Caramel sauce:

2 cups sugar
3 cups heavy whipping cream
1 stick (8 tablespoons) unsalted butter

Garnish:

6 scoops vanilla gelato (ice cream)
Powdered sugar
Fresh mint leaves

Peel the pears and cut in half. Remove the seeds and core. In a large pot over medium-high heat, combine the white wine, water, cinnamon, sugar, and lemon zest and juice. Slice the vanilla bean open and scrape out the inside. Add both the insides and the bean to the liquid. Bring to a boil. When boiling, add the pears and poach for 10 minutes. Remove pears and liquid from heat and let cool. Remove the pears and pat dry. Slice the pears thinly, retaining the original shape of the pear. Set aside.

To make the marzipan: Combine the almond powder, sugar, vanilla, and orange blossom water in a food processor. Mix while adding the egg whites, one at a time. Remove marzipan from food processor and set aside.

Preheat the oven to 350°F. Cut the puff pastry dough into twelve 5 x 3-inch oval pieces. Place six of these pieces atop wax paper on a baking sheet. Take the remaining six pieces and cut a smaller oval out of the center, leaving a hole with a 1/2-inch dough frame. Brush the six whole oval pieces of dough on the baking sheet with beaten egg. Place a cut-out pastry dough frame on top of each whole, egg-coated piece. Pat lightly to make sure the two pieces are stuck together. Place 1 teaspoon of marzipan in the center of each tart. Place one prepared sliced half pear on top of the marzipan for each tart. Brush entire top of each tart with egg. Bake for 15–20 minutes, or until golden. Let cool.

To make the caramel sauce: In a large pot over low heat, caramelize the sugar until it browns (do not burn). Add the cream, a little at a time. Stir and let cook over low heat until cream and sugar are well combined. Add the butter and mix until smooth.

Spoon 4 tablespoons of caramel sauce onto six serving plates. Swirl to cover base of entire plate. Place a pear tart off to one side of each plate and complement with one scoop of vanilla gelato. Sprinkle with powdered sugar and garnish gelato with a mint leaf.

Renaud's Patisserie & Bistro

3315 State Street, Santa Barbara
(805) 569-2400
www.renaudsbakery.com
Owners: Renaud and Nicole Gonthier

Ooh là là is what you will be saying when you try one of the creative pastries or other delicious dishes at Renaud's Patisserie & Bistro. In 2008 the husband-and-wife team of Renaud and Nicole Gonthier came up with a simple concept: excellent food and fresh French pastries. With more than twenty years of culinary and pastry experience, Renaud was eager to bring some French flair to Santa Barbara, and so the team quietly opened Renaud's Patisserie & Bistro in Loreto Plaza.

Today, the small-yet-busy Patisserie & Bistro shows no signs of slowing down. Now with two locations (the other is in Arlington Plaza), Renaud's has expanded its menu to include organic, cage-free, and grain-fed egg dishes, Renaud's signature breakfasts, and daily lunch specials that also include fresh, organic ingredients, such as the cheese ravioleties, quiche lorraine, and ratatouille tartines.

As for the town's locals, most come to Renaud's for the buttery croissants (try the almond), the amazing pastries, and fresh brewed coffee.

"I hope you will enjoy the madeleine and macaroon recipes (featured here)," says Chef Renaud. "They are as fun to eat as they are to make!"

MADELEINES

SERVES 6

2 sticks salted butter
2 eggs
1 cup self-rising flour
1 cup sugar
Chocolate chips (optional), for garnish
Chopped nuts (optional), for garnish

Preheat the oven to 400°F.

Melt the butter in a pan or in the microwave, and let cool. Beat the eggs in a bowl, and add the flour and sugar. Stir until the mixture is smooth. Add the warm butter and stir again until folded in.

Fill madeleine cookie molds (coated with butter) 2/3 full with the batter. (The molds come with 6 or 12 cavities. If yours has 12 cavities, you might need to double the recipe to fill all of them.)

Bake for 4 minutes, then lower the oven temperature to 350°F and bake for another 4 minutes. When done, the madeleines will be golden brown with a clear bump in the middle.

Remove from oven, let cool, and serve on individual serving plates. You can add chocolate chips and chopped nuts if you like.

Parisien Chocolate Macaroons with Chocolate Garnish

SERVES 6 TO 8

Macaroons:

2¼ cups almond flour

2 cups confectioner's sugar

⅓ cup cocoa

6 or 7 egg whites (depending on size of egg), divided

1 cup sugar

Chocolate garnish:

2 cups cream

2½ cups semisweet chocolate

1 stick butter, diced

Preheat the oven to 350°F. Combine the almond flour, confectioner's sugar, and cocoa, and then sift them together. Whisk 4 egg whites. Thicken the whisked egg whites by whisking in the sugar, and then fold in the almond flour mixture and the remaining nonwhisked egg whites. Fold the mixture multiple times to make sure the ingredients are fully incorporated.

Use a piping bag and pipe mixture in circles (roughly the size of a half dollar) onto a Silpat baking mat on a flat sheet pan (if you don't have a Silpat, pipe the mixture directly onto a greased baking sheet). Bake for 3 minutes, or until the macaroon bottoms are flat and crisp. Lower the oven temperature to 300°F and bake for an additional 6 minutes.

To make the chocolate garnish, bring the cream to a boil. Remove from heat and add chocolate, stirring until chocolate melts. Fold in the butter and stir until smooth. Using a piping bag, pipe the chocolate garnish onto one side of half of the macaroon shells and cover each with another macaroon shell.

THE VINEYARD HOUSE

3631 SAGUNTO STREET, SANTA YNEZ
(805) 688-2886
WWW.THEVINEYARDHOUSE.COM
OWNER: JIM SOBEL

The historic Vineyard House—formerly a blacksmith home—has been serving up regional cuisine to residents and visitors to the Santa Ynez Valley since 1907.

An infusion of Victorian craftsmanship and casual elegance, the Vineyard House stands alone on Sagunto Street, with its magnificent landscape and manicured lawns, lush flower gardens, and tranquil patios. This charming little spot is the perfect setting for lunch, dinner, or Sunday brunch, and the Vineyard House offers diners two cozy indoor rooms, along with two spacious outside decks for those preferring to soak up the California sunshine.

After a long day of wine tasting or exploring the peaceful valley, many end up at the Vineyard House, which offers a bevy of salads, soups, burgers, pizzas, and sandwiches,

including the popular grilled chicken and brie sandwich, the classic Reuben, and an albacore tuna salad sandwich. Dinner specials are often simmered venison with local tomatillos and Anaheim chiles, tender pork with fresh tomatillo broth and crispy corn tortillas, and a Cajun flatiron steak with roasted potatoes and red peppers.

But it's the desserts that have people really licking their lips. The Vineyard House's signature Macadamia Nut Banana Foster (featured here) and the Molten Chocolate Cake with a Dark Cherry Brandy Sauce (also featured) are just two of the delicious treats served to Vineyard guests. Other tempting treats include chocolate walnut brownies, cobblers using the finest berries from local fields and orchards, and a deliciously rich and creamy cheesecake, which the restaurant serves in various flavors.

Molten Chocolate Cake
with Dark Cherry Brandy Sauce

SERVES 6

Dark cherry brandy sauce:

1 16-ounce can dark cherries in syrup
¼ cup red wine
2 tablespoons brandy
¼ cup sugar
½ cinnamon stick

Molten chocolate cake:

1½ sticks (12 tablespoons) butter
1 cup chocolate chips
¾ cup sugar
¼ cup plus 2 tablespoons cocoa powder
4 eggs
8 egg yolks
⅛ cup all-purpose flour

Vanilla bean ice cream
Whipped cream, for garnish
Fresh mint, for garnish

To make the dark cherry brandy sauce: Combine the cherries (with syrup), red wine, brandy, sugar, and cinnamon stick in a heavy saucepan over medium-high heat. Whisk well to combine. Bring to a boil, and then reduce heat to low. Simmer until the sauce is reduced by half and thick enough to coat the back of a spoon. Set aside and allow to cool to room temperature.

Preheat the oven to 375°F. In a heavy saucepan over low heat, melt the butter and chocolate chips, and whisk to combine. In a stainless mixing bowl, combine the sugar and cocoa powder. Whisk to combine, and then whisk the mixture into the melted butter and chocolate chips. Whisk in the eggs and egg yolks. Whisk in the flour.

Butter six (6-ounce) ovenproof ramekins. Divide the mixture equally among the individual ramekins. Bake until the cakes rise and are slightly soft to the touch, about 20 minutes. Check by inserting a toothpick; the toothpick should come out moist from the liquid center. Remove from oven and wrap a cloth napkin or dishtowel around the ramekins so they can be handled. Run a knife around the outsides of the cakes to loosen from the sides.

Invert the cakes onto individual serving plates. Top with a scoop of vanilla bean ice cream and a dollop of whipped cream. Garnish with the dark cherry brandy sauce and a sprig of mint.

Macadamia Nut Banana Foster

SERVES 1 OR 2

1 banana
½ stick (4 tablespoons) butter
⅓ cup brown sugar, loosely packed
¼ cup dark rum
4 ounces vanilla bean ice cream
Whipped cream, for garnish
1 ounce crushed macadamia nuts

Peel the banana and slice it lengthwise. Melt the butter in a medium skillet over medium-high heat. Add the banana and sauté for about 1 minute. Turn over and continue sautéing for 30 seconds. Add the brown sugar and rum.

Carefully tilt pan towards a stove flame (such as a gas burner) and carefully ignite rum (the flames will be almost two feet high, so be cautious!). Swirl the pan so the butter, brown sugar, and rum mix well together (the mixture will be very hot and bubbly). Cook for just another minute.

Transfer the banana to an oblong serving dish. Place a large scoop of vanilla bean ice cream in the middle, and pour the butter–brown sugar–rum mixture over the banana and ice cream. Garnish with a dollop of whipped cream on each side of the ice cream and sprinkle the macadamia nuts over the top.

SANTA YNEZ

An alluring combination of cowboy swagger and proud western history, the turn-of-the-twentieth-century town of Santa Ynez is at the top of the list for visitors to the Santa Ynez Valley. Just 30 miles from Santa Barbara, the town's attractions include to-die-for scenery, with golden and sage-green oak-studded hills, acres of vineyards and dozens of wineries, historic sites and outdoor activities from horseback riding and hiking to cycling and boating. And for folks feeling lucky, the nearby Chumash Casino Resort features 24-7 gaming.

The town's rich history is on display at the Santa Ynez Valley Historical Museum & Carriage House, with eight intriguing rooms of memorabilia ranging from Chumash Indian artifacts through twentieth-century ranching days and the largest collection of horse-drawn vehicles and accessories west of the Mississippi.

Visitors continue the step back in time with refreshment at a historic saloon, then choose from a variety of restaurants, from gourmet to Italian to steakhouse. Current cowboys bunk at a luxury AAA four-diamond inn or a delightful bed and breakfast. Popular wineries include Gainey Vineyard, producing world-class wines for more than twenty-five years, and Sunstone Vineyards & Winery, with 56 acres of organic vineyards.

Metric US Approximate Equivalents

LIQUID INGREDIENTS

Metric	U.S. Measures	Metric	U.S. Measures
1.23 ml	¼ tsp.	29.57 ml	2 tbsp.
2.36 ml	½ tsp.	44.36 ml	3 tbsp.
3.70 ml	¾ tsp.	59.15 ml	¼ cup
4.93 ml	1 tsp.	118.30 ml	½ cup
6.16 ml	1¼ tsp.	236.59 ml	1 cup
7.39 ml	1½ tsp.	473.18 ml	2 cups or 1 pt.
8.63 ml	1¾ tsp.	709.77 ml	3 cups
9.86 ml	2 tsp.	946.36 ml	4 cups or 1 qt.
14.79 ml	1 tbsp.	3.79 l	4 qts. or 1 gal.

DRY INGREDIENTS

Metric	U.S. Measures	Metric	U.S. Measures
2 (1.8) g	1/16 oz.	80 g	2⅘ oz.
3½ (3.5) g	⅛ oz.	85 (84.9) g	3 oz.
7 (7.1) g	¼ oz.	100 g	3½ oz.
15 (14.2) g	½ oz.	115 (113.2) g	4 oz.
21 (21.3) g	¾ oz.	125 g	4½ oz.
25 g	⅞ oz.	150 g	5¼ oz.
30 (28.3) g	1 oz.	250 g	8⅞ oz.
50 g	1¾ oz.	454 g	1 lb. (16 oz.)
60 (56.6) g	2 oz.	500 g	1 livre (17⅗ oz.)

Index

Photo Credits

About the Author

James O. Fraioli (pronounced FRAY-o-lee) is an award-winning cookbook author. He has written seventeen titles, with additional cookbooks currently in production. Fraioli's cookbooks have garnered numerous literary awards and have been featured on the Food Network and *The Ellen DeGeneres Show* and given as gifts to members of the White House staff. The author is famed for teaming up with celebrity chefs and world-renowned restaurants to showcase the best the culinary world has to offer. Participating chefs over the years include James Beard award–winners John Ash, Tom Douglas, Bradley Ogden, Jacques Pépin, and Holly Smith, as well as Emeril Lagasse and Roy Yamaguchi. Fraioli's cookbooks have also been featured on dozens of national radio shows, including Martha Stewart Living Radio and Dining Around with Gene Burns. The author's beautiful and well-crafted 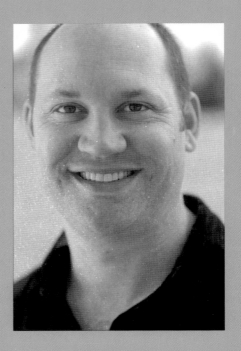 books, continually noted for their exceptional prose, high production values, exquisite photography, and savory subject matter, have received further praise from such periodicals as *Forbes Traveler, Reader's Digest,* the *San Francisco Chronicle,* and the *New York Times.* Visit him on the web at www.culinarybookcreations.com.